LITTLE
SCIENCE,
BIG
SCIENCE

DEREK J. DE SOLLA PRICE

COLUMBIA
UNIVERSITY PRESS
NEW YORK AND LONDON

THE
GEORGE B. PEGRAM
LECTURES

SCIENCE PLAYS such an important role in today's world that opportunities for reflective appraisals of the interaction between science and other aspects of our society should be cultivated. To this end the Trustees of Associated Universities, Inc., established the annual George B. Pegram Lectureship at Brookhaven National Laboratory. Each lecture series is given over a period of about two weeks during which the lecturer resides at the Laboratory. This arrangement provides for him many opportunities for formal and informal contacts with the staff as well as a period of freedom from other duties.

The lectureship was named to honor George Braxton Pegram (1877–1958), one of the most influential scientists of the nuclear age. He was Professor of Physics, Dean, and Vice President of Columbia University. He was instrumental in seeing that the government was aware of the potentialities of nuclear energy in the defense of the country. In 1946 he headed the Initiatory University Group which proposed that a regional center for research in the nuclear sciences be established in the New York area and thus played a key role in the establishment of Associated Universities, Inc., and the founding of Brookhaven National Laboratory. He received many awards

THE GEORGE B. PEGRAM LECTURES

and honorary degrees, the last of which was the Karl Taylor Compton gold medal for distinguished service in physics. George B. Pegram's lucid mind and gentle ways will be long remembered by those who knew him. This series in his honor has been established to further his conviction that the results of science can be made to serve the needs and hopes of mankind.

The previous Pegram Lecturers have been distinguished scientists who, from their various points of view, examined the impact of science and scientists on society. Professor Derek J. de Solla Price of Yale University, the fourth lecturer in the series, is a well-known historian of science who, in a sense, chose to look at the other side of the coin. His lectures, given June 19–29, 1962, deal with the sociology of science itself. Applying scientific methods to an investigation of the rapid growth of science, the changing role of scientific publications, and the evolution of scientific organizations, Dr. Price presents a fascinating analysis of problems which are central in the lives of today's scientists. His dual background as a physicist and a historian qualifies him uniquely for the task he has set himself.

The 1962 Pegram Lectureship Committee

GEORGE B. COLLINS

HERBERT J. KOUTS

IRVING J. POLK

HENRY QUASTLER

JAMES S. ROBERTSON

GERHART FRIEDLANDER, *Chairman*

PREFACE

PEGRAM LECTURERS are supposed to talk about science and its place in society. The ordinary way of doing this would be either to talk popular science or to adopt one of the various styles in humanistic discussion of the reactions between men and science. Previous lecturers in this series have given accounts of the content of space science and made excursions into the philosophy and the history of science. Although professionally my concern is with the history of science, I have a certain prehistoric past as a physicist, and this has led me to treat these lectures in what is, perhaps, an extraordinary way.

My goal is not discussion of the content of science or even a humanistic analysis of its relations. Rather, I want to clarify these more usual approaches by treating separately all the scientific analyses that may be made of science. Why should we not turn the tools of science on science itself? Why not measure and generalize, make hypotheses, and derive conclusions?

In lectures emanating from so large an atomic establishment as Brookhaven, it would be gratuitous to explain how science has become a crucial and very expensive part of man's activity. In the course of its growth to this condition, science has acquired a great deal of administration, organization, and politicking. These have evolved, for the most part, on an *ad hoc,* empirical basis. Most of the time I worry that there has been insufficient humanistic appraisal of the situation. In these lectures, I shall worry that we have not been sufficiently scientific in analyzing a whole set of regularities that can be dissected out before beginning to deal humanistically with those irregularities that occur because men are men, and not machines.

My approach will be to deal statistically, in a not very mathematical fashion, with general problems of the shape and size of science and the ground rules governing growth and behavior of science-in-the-large. That is to say, I shall not discuss any part of the detail of scientific discoveries, their use and interrelations. I shall not even discuss specific scientists. Rather, treating science as a measurable entity, I shall attempt to develop a calculus of scientific manpower, literature, talent, and expenditure on a national and on an international scale. From such a calculus we hope to analyze what it is that is essentially new in the present age of Big Science, distinguishing it from the former state of Little Science.

The method to be used is similar to that of thermodynamics, in which is discussed the behavior of a gas under various conditions of temperature and pressure. One does not fix one's gaze on a specific molecule called George, traveling at a specific velocity and being in a specific place at some given instant; one considers only an average of the total assemblage in which some molecules are faster than others, and in which they are spaced out randomly and moving in different directions. On the basis of such an impersonal average, useful

PREFACE

things can be said about the behavior of the gas * as a whole, and it is in this way that I want to discuss the analysis of science as a whole.

According to this metaphor, my first lecture is concerned with the volume of science, the second with the velocity distribution of its molecules, the third with the way in which the molecules interact with one another, and the fourth in deriving the political and social properties of this gas.

DEREK J. DE SOLLA PRICE

New Haven
November, 1962

* One must bear in mind that *gas* derives from the Greek *Khaos*, a perfectly general term for a chaos.

ACKNOWLEDGMENTS

I gratefully acknowledge the stimulus and help afforded by graduate students in my seminars at Yale University, the work and devotion of my research assistant, Miss Joy Day, and the intent literary vigilance of my good friend David Klein. Thanks are also due to Asger Aaboe for drawing many beautiful graphs. I am further indebted to Yale University Press for permission to reproduce figures from *Science Since Babylon* which I published with them in 1962; to the McGraw-Hill Book Company for permission to reproduce the graph on development of accelerators from M. S. Livingston and J. P. Blewett, *Particle Accelerators;* to the Addison-Wesley Publishing Company for the graph on growth of cities from G. K. Zipf, *Human Behavior and the Principle of Least Effort;* and to the Cambridge University Press for permission to use an adaption of a figure from D'Arcy W. Thompson, *Growth and Form.*

CONTENTS

How big are you, baby?
Why, don't you know,
You're only so big,
And there's still room to grow.

(NURSERY RHYME)

(1)

PROLOGUE TO
A SCIENCE
OF SCIENCE

DURING A MEETING at which a number of great physicists were
to give firsthand accounts of their epoch-making discoveries,
the chairman opened the proceedings with the remark: "Today
we are privileged to sit side-by-side with the giants on whose
shoulders we stand." [1] This, in a nutshell, exemplifies the peculiar immediacy of science, the recognition that so large a
proportion of everything scientific that has ever occurred
is happening now, within living memory. To put it another
way, using any reasonable definition of a scientist, we can
say that 80 to 90 percent of all the scientists that have ever
lived are alive now. Alternatively, any young scientist, starting

[1] Gerald Holton, "On the recent past of physics," *American Journal of
Physics*, 29 (December, 1961), 805. I should like to draw attention to
the fine study published while this work was in progress: Gerald Holton,
"Models for Understanding the Growth and Excellence of Scientific
Research," in S. R. Graubard and G. Holton, eds., *Excellence and
Leadership in a Democracy* (New York, Columbia University Press,
1962), 94–131, first published as "Scientific research and scholarship:
notes towards the design of proper scales," in *Proceedings of the American Academy of Arts and Sciences*, 91 (No. 2), 362–99 (*Daedalus*,
March, 1962). My work derives much from this previous publication,
though its author and I do not always agree in detail in the conclusions
we derive from the statistical data.

now and looking back at the end of his career upon a normal life span, will find that 80 to 90 percent of all scientific work achieved by the end of the period will have taken place before his very eyes, and that only 10 to 20 percent will antedate his experience.

So strong and dominant a characteristic of science is this immediacy, that one finds it at the root of many attitudes taken by scientist and layman toward modern science. It is what makes science seem essentially modern and contemporaneous. As a historian of science, I find myself doing annual battle to justify and uphold the practice of spending more than half our time on the period before Newton, whereas every contemporary scientist around knows that what really counts is science since Einstein.

Because the science we have now so vastly exceeds all that has gone before, we have obviously entered a new age that has been swept clear of all but the basic traditions of the old. Not only are the manifestations of modern scientific hardware so monumental that they have been usefully compared with the pyramids of Egypt and the great cathedrals of medieval Europe, but the national expenditures of manpower and money on it have suddenly made science a major segment of our national economy. The large-scale character of modern science, new and shining and all-powerful, is so apparent that the happy term "Big Science" has been coined to describe it.[2] Big Science is so new that many of us can remember its beginnings. Big Science is so large that many of us begin to worry about the sheer mass of the monster we have created.

[2] Alvin M. Weinberg, "Impact of large-scale science on the United States," *Science,* 134 (July 21, 1961), 164. I am indebted to this paper for many ideas. See also further comments by Weinberg in "The Federal Laboratories and science education," *Science,* 136 (April 6, 1962), 27.

Big Science is so different from the former state of affairs that we can look back, perhaps nostalgically, at the Little Science that was once our way of life.

If we are to understand how to live and work in the age newly dawned, it is clearly necessary to appreciate the nature of the transition from Little Science to Big Science. It is only too easy to dramatize the change and see the differences with reckless naïveté. But how much truth is there in the picture of the Little Scientist as the lone, long-haired genius, moldering in an attic or basement workshop, despised by society as a nonconformist, existing in a state of near poverty, motivated by the flame burning within him? And what about the corresponding image of the Big Scientist? Is he honored in Washington, sought after by all the research corporations of the "Boston ring road," part of an elite intellectual brotherhood of co-workers, arbiters of political as well as technological destiny? And the basis of the change—was it an urgent public reaction to the first atomic explosion and the first national shocks of military missiles and satellites? Did it all happen very quickly, with historical roots no deeper in time than the Manhattan Project, Cape Canaveral rocketry, the discovery of penicillin, and the invention of radar and electronic computers?

I think one can give a flat "No" in answer to all these questions. The images are too naïvely conceived, and the transition from Little Science to Big Science was less dramatic and more gradual than appears at first. For one thing, it is clear that Little Science contained many elements of the grandiose. And, tucked away in some academic corners, modern Big Science probably contains shoestring operations by unknown pioneers who are starting lines of research that will be of decisive interest by 1975. It is the brave exception rather than the rule that key break-throughs are heralded at birth as important work done by important people.

Historically, there have been numerous big national efforts: the great observatories of Ulugh Beg in Samarkand in the fifteenth century, of Tycho Brahe on his island of Hven in the sixteenth century, and of Jai Singh in India in the seventeenth century, each of which absorbed sensibly large fractions of the available resources of their nations. As international efforts, there were the gigantic expeditions of the eighteenth century to observe the transits of Venus. And, as large-scale hardware, there were the huge electrical machines, produced most notably in Holland in the eighteenth century, machines that in their time seemed to stretch man's scientific engineering to its ultimate capability and to give him the power to manufacture the most extreme physical forces of the universe, rivaling the very lightning and perhaps providing keys to the nature of matter and of life itself. In a way, our dreams for modern accelerators pale by comparison.

But let us not be distracted by history. What shall concern us is not so much the offering of counterexamples to show that Little Science was sometimes big, and Big Science little, but rather a demonstration that such change as has occurred has been remarkably gradual. To get at this we must begin our analysis of science by taking measurements, and in this case it is even more difficult than usual to make such determinations and find out what they mean.

Our starting point will be the empirical statistical evidence drawn from many numerical indicators of the various fields and aspects of science. All of these show with impressive consistency and regularity that if any sufficiently large segment of science is measured in any reasonable way, the normal mode of growth is exponential. That is to say, science grows at compound interest, multiplying by some fixed amount in equal periods of time. Mathematically, the law of exponential growth follows from the simple condition that at any time the rate of growth is proportional to the size of the population or to the total magnitude already achieved—the bigger a thing is, the faster it grows. In this respect it agrees with the common natural law of growth governing the number of human beings in the population of the world or of a particular country, the number of fruit flies growing in a colony in a bottle, or the number of miles of railroad built in the early industrial revolution.

It might at first seem as if establishing such an empirical law of growth for science was neither unexpected nor significant. The law has, however, several remarkable features, and from it a number of powerful conclusions can be drawn. Indeed, it is so far-reaching that I have no hesitation in suggesting it as the fundamental law of any analysis of science.

Its most surprising and significant feature is that, unlike most pieces of curve-fitting, the empirical law holds true with high accuracy over long periods of time. Even with a somewhat careless and uncritical choice of the index taken as a measure, one has little trouble in showing that general exponential growth has been maintained for two or three centuries. The law therefore, though at this stage still merely empirical, has a status immediately more significant than the usual short-term economic time series. This leads one to a strong suspicion that the law is more than empirical—and that with suitable definitions of the indices that grow exponentially, one may show, as we later shall, that there is a reasonable theoretical basis for such a law.

A second important feature of the growth of science is that it is surprisingly rapid however it is measured. An exponential increase is best characterized by stating the time required for a doubling in size or for a tenfold increase.[3] Now, depending on what one measures and how, the crude size of science in manpower or in publications tends to double within a period of 10 to 15 years. The 10-year period emerges from those catchall measures that do not distinguish low-grade work from high but adopt a basic, minimal definition of science; the 15-year period results when one is more selective, counting only some more stringent definition of published scientific work and those who produce it. If this stringency is increased so that only scientific work of *very* high quality is counted, then the doubling period is drawn out so that it approaches about 20 years.

The following list shows the order of magnitudes of an assortment of measurable and estimatable doubling times and shows how rapidly the growth of science and technology has been outstripping that of the size of the population and of our nonscientific institutions.

100 years

    Entries in dictionaries of national biography

50 years

    Labor force
    Population
    Number of universities

20 years

    Gross National Product
    Important discoveries

[3] It is easy enough to convert from one to the other by noting, as a rough approximation, that 10 doubling periods correspond to a factor of 1024, or about 3 tenfolding periods.

Important physicists
Number of chemical elements known
Accuracy of instruments
College entrants/1000 population

15 years

B.A., B.Sc.
Scientific journals
Membership of scientific institutes
Number of chemical compounds known
Number of scientific abstracts, all fields

10 years

Number of asteroids known
Literature in theory of determinants
Literature in non-Euclidean geometry
Literature in x rays
Literature in experimental psychology
Number of telephones in United States
Number of engineers in United States
Speed of transportation
Kilowatt-hours of electricity

5 years

Number of overseas telephone calls
Magnetic permeability of iron

1½ years

Million electron volts of accelerators

Bearing in mind the long period of validity of exponential growth, let us note that a 15-year doubling time extended over three centuries of growth corresponds to an increase of 20 powers of two, or a factor of about one million. Thus, in the interval from 1660 to the present day, such indices of the size of science should have increased by the order of a million. To offer the soundest explanation of the scientific and industrial revolutions is to posit that this is indeed what has been happening.

Just after 1660, the first national scientific societies in the modern tradition were founded; they established the first scientific periodicals, and scientists found themselves beginning to write scientific papers instead of the books that hitherto had been their only outlets. We have now a world list of some 50,000 scientific periodicals (Fig. 1) that have been founded, of which about 30,000 are still being published; these have produced a world total of about six million scientific papers (Fig. 2) and an increase at the approximate rate of at least half a million a year.[4] In general, the same applies to scientific manpower. Whereas in the mid-seventeenth century there were a few scientific men—a denumerable few who were countable and namable—there is now in the United States alone a population on the order of a million with scientific and technical degrees (Fig. 3). What is more, the same exponential law accounts quite well for all the time in between. The present million came through intermediate stages of 100,000 in 1900, 10,000 in 1850, and 1000 in 1800. In terms of magnitude alone, the transition from Little Science to Big Science has been steady—or at least has had only minor periodic fluctuations similar to those of the stock market—and it has followed a law of exponential growth with the time rates previously stated.

Thus, the steady doubling every 15 years or so that has brought us into the present scientific age has produced the peculiar immediacy that enables us to say that so much of

---

[4] For a more detailed discussion of this see Derek J. de Solla Price, *Science Since Babylon* (New Haven, Yale University Press, 1961), Chapter 5.

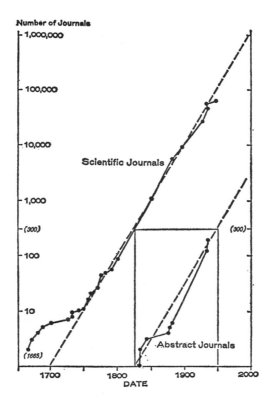

Fig. 1. TOTAL NUMBER OF SCIENTIFIC JOURNALS AND ABSTRACT
JOURNALS FOUNDED, AS A FUNCTION OF DATE

Note that abstracts begin when the population of journals is approximately 300. Numbers recorded here are for journals founded, rather than those surviving; for all periodicals containing any "science" rather than for "strictly scientific" journals. Tighter definitions might reduce the absolute numbers by an order of magnitude, but the general trend remains constant for all definitions. From Derek J. de Solla Price, *Science Since Babylon* (New Haven, Yale University Press, 1961).

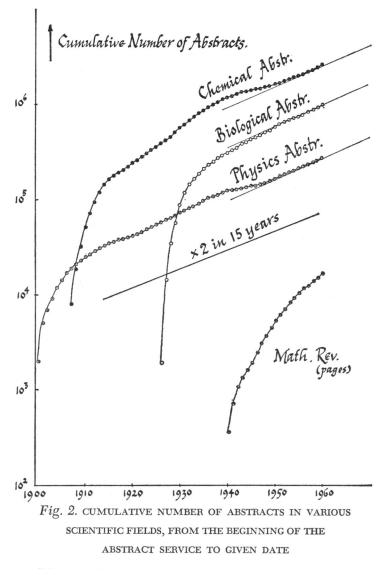

Fig. 2. CUMULATIVE NUMBER OF ABSTRACTS IN VARIOUS
SCIENTIFIC FIELDS, FROM THE BEGINNING OF THE
ABSTRACT SERVICE TO GIVEN DATE

It will be noted that after an initial period of rapid expansion to a stable
growth rate, the number of abstracts increases exponentially, doubling
in approximately 15 years.

science is current and that so many of its practitioners are alive. If we start with the law that the number of living scientists doubles in, let us say, 15 years, then in any interval of 15 years there will come into being as many scientists again as in the whole of time preceding. But at any moment there coexists a body of scientists produced not over 15 years but over an interval nearer to the 45 years separating average date of arrival at the research front from average date of retirement from active scientific work. Thus, for every one person born before such a period of 45 years, we now have one born in the first doubling period, two in the second, and four in the third. There are, then, about seven scientists alive for every eight that have ever been, a fraction of 87½ percent; let us call this a coefficient of immediacy. One may calculate this exactly by using actuarial mortality tables, but in fact the result is not much altered by this because the doubling period of science is so much less than the average working life of a scientist.

For a doubling period of 10 years, the corresponding coefficient of immediacy is about 96 percent; for a doubling time of 20 years, about 81 percent. Thus, even if one admits only the general form of the growth function and the order of magnitude of its time constant, these account for the feeling that most of the great scientists are still with us, and that the greater part of scientific work has been produced within living memory, within the span of the present generation of scientists. Furthermore, one can emphasize the principle by remarking that some time between the next decade and the one after we shall have produced as much scientific work and as many scientists as in the whole of time up to the present.

What we have said so far is by now well known and reason-

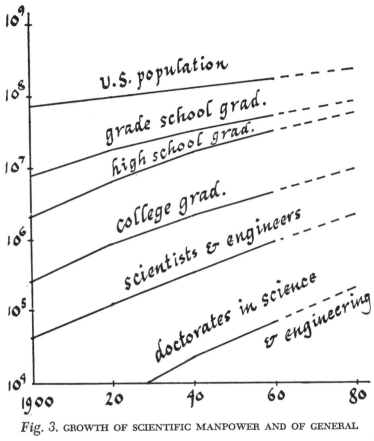

Fig. 3. GROWTH OF SCIENTIFIC MANPOWER AND OF GENERAL POPULATION IN THE UNITED STATES

It may be seen that the more highly qualified the manpower, the greater has been its growth rate. It will also be noted that there appears a distinct tendency for the curves to turn toward a ceiling value running parallel with the population curve.

ably well agreed upon by those who speculate about science for fun or high policy. I should like to extend these results, however, in a couple of ways that may suggest that this outlook requires revision. In the first place, speaking in terms of a "coefficient of immediacy" can be misleading. Let us compare the figures just found with the conjectural figures for world population.

At the beginning of the Christian Era, the human race numbered about 250 million; it grew slowly and erratically, differently in different places and at different times, and reached a figure of 550 million by the mid-seventeenth century. It has grown at an ever-increasing pace, so that today there are about 3000 million people, and it looks as though that number will double every 40 to 50 years. If we reckon about 20 years to a generation, there must have been at least 60,000 millions of people, and thus only about 5 percent of those who have lived since the beginning of our era are alive now. If we count all those who lived before the time of Christ, the fraction will be smaller; if we count only those who have lived since the mid-seventeenth century, it will be a little more than 10 percent. Making due allowance for changing mortalities and age of child-bearing will not, I feel, materially alter the qualitative result that the human population is far from immediate in the sense that science is.

Even if we accept the gloomy prognostications of those who talk about the admittedly serious problem of the population explosion, it would apparently take about another half-century—some time after the year 2000—before we could claim that 50 percent of all the human beings that have lived were at that moment alive. Most of the persons that have ever lived are *dead*, and, in the sense that this will continue to be so, they will stay dead. One might conclude, since the rate of growth of entries in the great dictionaries of national biographies shows a fairly constant proportion to the population at various dates, that most of the great or worthy persons of the world are dead. That is why *history* is a subject rather different from *history of science*. There is much more past to live in if you discuss politics and wars than if you discuss science.

The immediacy of science needs a comparison of this sort before one can realize that it implies an explosion of science dwarfing that of the population, and indeed all other explosions of nonscientific human growth. Roughly speaking, every doubling of the population has produced at least three doublings of the number of scientists, so that the size of science is eight times what it was and the number of scientists per million population has multiplied by four. Mankind's per capita involvement with science has thus been growing much more rapidly than the population.

A second clarification, one of crucial importance, must be made concerning the immediacy and growth of modern science. We have already shown that the 80- to 90-percent currency of modern science is a direct result of an exponential growth that has been steady and consistent for a long time. It follows that this result, true now, must also have been true *at all times in the past,* back to the eighteenth century and perhaps even as far back as the late seventeenth. In 1900, in 1800, and perhaps in 1700, one could look back and say that most of the scientists that have ever been are alive now, and most of what is known has been determined within living memory. In that respect, surprised though we may be to find it so, the scientific world is no different now from what it has always been since the seventeenth century. Science has always been modern; it has always been exploding into the population, always on the brink of its expansive revolution. Scientists have always felt themselves to be awash in a sea of scientific literature that augments in each decade as much as in all times before.

It is not difficult to find good historical authority for this feeling in all epochs. In the nineteenth century we have Charles Babbage in England and Nathaniel Bowditch in the United States bitterly deploring the lack of recognition of the new scientific era that had just burst upon them. In the eighteenth century there were the first furtive moves toward special journals and abstracts in a vain attempt to halt or at least rationalize the rising tide of publications; there is Sir Humphrey Davy, whose habit it was to throw books away after reading on the principle that no man could ever have the time or occasion to read the same thing twice. Even in the seventeenth century, we must not forget that the motivating purpose of the *Philosophical Transactions of the Royal Society* and the *Journal des Sçavans* was *not* the publishing of new scientific papers so much as the monitoring and digesting of the learned publications and letters that now were too much for one man to cope with in his daily reading and correspondence.[5]

The principle of more than 80 percent being contemporaneous is clearly sufficient to cast out any naïve idea that sheer change in scale has led us from Little Science to Big Science. If we are to distinguish the present phase as something new, something different from the perception of a burgeoning science

---

[5] An excellent historical account of the birth of scientific journals is given by David A. Kronick, *A History of Scientific and Technical Periodicals* (New York, Scarecrow Press, Inc., 1962).

that was common to Maxwell, to Franklin, and to Newton, then we cannot rest our case on the rate of growth alone. A science that has advanced steadily through more than five orders of magnitude in more than 250 years is not going to be upset by a mere additional single order of magnitude such as we have experienced within the last few decades of the present century.

As a side point one may note that the constancy of this phenomenon of immediacy is typical of many other constancies in science that make it meaningful and useful to pursue the history of science even though most of our past is alive. What we must do in the humanistic and the scientific analyses of science is search out such constancies of scientific method, of public reaction, of the use of mathematical models or euphoric hardware or the ground rules of manpower and motivation, and apply them to our criticism and understanding of this science that seems so essentially modern and out of all relation to Archimedes or Galileo or Boyle or Benjamin Franklin. If we honor a Boyle for his law, or a Planck for his constant, this is largely accidental hero worship; more important to us than the names of those who have quarried a slab of immortality is their having done so in a manner which notably illustrates the constant and seemingly eternal way in which these things have been going on. To take an early example such as Galileo, seen in all its historical perspective, is in many ways more efficient than choosing a recent example such as Oppenheimer, though Galileo can tell us nothing of the content of modern atomic physics as can Oppenheimer.

To return to our main point, if the sheer growth of science in its exponential climb is *not* admissible as an explanation for the transition from Little Science to Big Science, we are left in a quandary. To escape from it one may be tempted at first to deny that there has been any such radical transformation of the state of science. This is amply belied by the fact that since World War II we have been worried about questions of scientific manpower and literature, government spending, and military power in ways that seem quite different, not merely in scale, from all that went before.

Even if one admits that new things are happening and that Big Science differs not merely in scale from Little Science, one might still maintain that it was the cataclysmic changes associated with World War II that initiated us into the new era and produced all the major changes. Quite unexpectedly, one can show from the statistical studies we have been using to measure the pure growth that the influence of the war on scientific manpower and literature seems only to have been the production of a temporary perturbation that extended for its duration.

For this interval it is not possible to use the indices one might use before or after; manpower may be in military service, publication may be suppressed for secrecy. Yet it is apparent that the exponential increase after the war is identical with that before (Fig. 4). This is a strong result, for it shows that the percentage increase per annum is the same before and after the war and, therefore, if there is any constancy about the way in which scientific papers generate new scientific papers and researchers generate new classes of researchers, there cannot have been any great loss or gain to science during the war. With the exception only of a sidewise displacement of the curve due to secrecy loss, science is just where it would have been, statistically speaking, and is growing at the same rate as if there had been no war. The order of events might have been different, the political implications perhaps grossly so, but there is some reason for taking a fatalistic line that it was in the nature of things for accelerator laboratories to grow as large as Brookhaven, and missile establishments as large as Cape Canaveral, and that had there been no Manhattan Project there might still have been a Sputnik. The

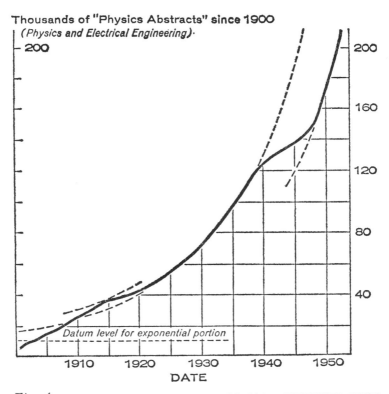

Thousands of "Physics Abstracts" since 1900
(Physics and Electrical Engineering)

Fig. 4. TOTAL NUMBER OF PHYSICS ABSTRACTS PUBLISHED SINCE
JANUARY 1, 1900

The full curve gives the total, and the broken curve represents the exponential approximation. Parallel curves are drawn to enable the effect of the wars to be illustrated. From Derek J. de Solla Price, *Science Since Babylon* (New Haven, Yale University Press, 1961).

war looms as a huge milepost, but it stands at the side of a straight road of exponential growth.

If, then, we are to analyze the peculiarities of Big Science, we must search for whatever there is other than the steady hand-in-hand climb of all the indices of science through successive orders of magnitude. There are, I propose, two quite different types of general statistical phenomena of science-in-the-large. On the one hand, although we have the over-all picture of a steady exponential growth with this amazingly short time constant of about 15 years, not all things are growing at precisely this rate; some are faster, others slower, though all of them outpace the growth of the population. On the other hand, we have the possibility that the exponential law of growth may be beginning to break down.

It is just possible that the tradition of more than 250 years represents a sort of adolescent stage during which every half-century science grew out of its order of magnitude, donned a new suit of clothes, and was ready to expand again. Perhaps now a post-adolescent quiescence has set in, and such exuberant growth has slowed down and is about to stop upon the attainment of adult stature. After all, five orders of magnitude is rather a lot. Scientists and engineers are now a couple of percent of the labor force of the United States, and the annual expenditure on research and development is about the same fraction of the Gross National Product. It is clear that we cannot go up another two orders of magnitude as we have climbed the last five. If we did, we should have two scientists for every man, woman, child, and dog in the population, and we should spend on them twice as much money as we had. Scientific doomsday is therefore less than a century distant.

At a later point I shall treat separately the problem of

growths at rates different from that of basic exponential increase. We shall consider such growths as slowly changing statistical distributions of the indices rather than as separate rates of increase. Thus, for example, if the number of science Ph.D's were doubling every 15 years, and the number of good ones only every 20 years, the quota of Ph.D's per good physicist would be doubling only every 60 years, a change so slow that we can count it out of the scientific explosion. I shall show also, from the statistical distribution, that it is reasonable on theoretical grounds to suppose that the doubling time of one measure might be a multiple of the period for some other index. This treatment, however, requires a closer look at what is actually being measured and must be deferred until further results have been achieved from the study of the crude shape of exponential growth.

Moreover, the "normal" law of growth that we have been considering thus far describes, in fact, a most abnormal state of events. In the real world things do not grow and grow until they reach infinity. Rather, exponential growth eventually reaches some limit, at which the process must slacken and stop before reaching absurdity. This more realistic function is also well known as the logistic curve, and it exists in several slightly different mathematical forms. Again, at this stage of ignorance of science in analysis, we are not particularly concerned with the detailed mathematics or precise formulation of measurements. For the first approximation (or, more accurately, the zeroth-order approximation) let it suffice to consider the general trend of the growth.

The logistic curve is limited by a floor—that is, by the base value of the index of growth, usually zero—and by a ceiling, which is the ultimate value of the growth beyond which it cannot go in its accustomed fashion (Fig. 5). In its typical pattern, growth starts exponentially and maintains this pace to a point almost halfway between floor and ceiling, where it has an inflection. After this, the pace of growth declines so that the curve continues toward the ceiling in a manner symmetrical with the way in which it climbed from the floor to the midpoint. This symmetry is an interesting property; rarely in nature does one

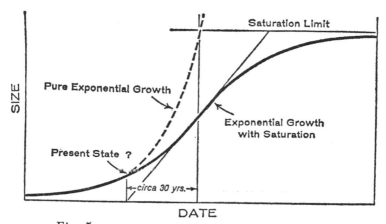

Fig. 5. GENERAL FORM OF THE LOGISTIC CURVE

From Derek J. de Solla Price, *Science Since Babylon* (New Haven, Yale University Press, 1961).

find asymmetrical logistic curves that use up one more parameter to describe them. Nature appears to be parsimonious with her parameters of growth.

Because of the symmetry so often found in the logistic curves that describe the growth of organisms, natural and manmade, measuring science or measuring the number of fruit flies in a bottle, the width of the curve can be simply defined. Mathematically, of course, the curve extends to infinity in both directions along the time axis. For convenience we measure the width of the midregion cut off by the tangent at the point of inflection, a quantity corresponding to the distance between the quartiles on a standard curve of error or its integral. This midregion may be shown necessarily to extend on either side of the center for a distance equal to about three of the doubling periods of the exponential growth.

Thus, for example, if we have a beanstalk that doubles in height every day, there will exist a midperiod of about six days during which the beanstalk will leave its juvenile exponential growth and settle down to an adult life of stability in length (Fig. 6). The only question is one of how much free and exponential growth is allowed before the decelerative period sets in. For the beanstalk, the midpoint of growth occurs only about

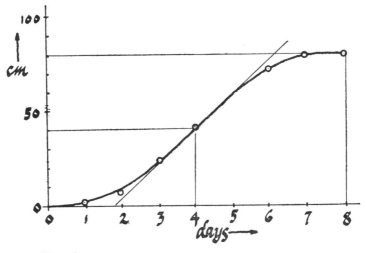

Fig. 6. GROWTH IN LENGTH OF A BEANSTALK AS A
FUNCTION OF AGE

Adapted from D'Arcy W. Thompson, *Growth and Form* (Cambridge, England, Cambridge University Press, 1948), p. 116, Fig. 20.

four days after the onset of the process, so that there is but one day of relatively free growth, and final length is attained after seven days. Note that the analysis involved no knowledge about the height of the curve from floor to ceiling. True, we made a statement about the date of the midpoint—it occurred after four days of growth—but we could equally well have noted that the exponential growth, short-lived in this case, extends only for the first day, and from this it would follow that three more doublings must bring it to the midpoint, and a further three to senescence.

Now, with no stronger assumption than has been made about the previously regular exponential growth with a doubling period of 10 to 15 years, we may deduce, as we have, that the existence of a ceiling is plausible since we should otherwise reach absurd conditions at the end of another century. Given the existence of such a limit, we must conclude that our exponential growth is merely the beginning of a logistic curve in other guise. Moreover, it is seen that as soon as one enters the midregion near the inflection—that period of secession from accustomed conditions of exponential growth—then another 30 to 45 years will elapse before the exact midpoint between floor and ceiling is reached. An equal period thereafter, the curve will effectively have reached its limit. Thus, without reference to the present state of affairs or any estimate of just when and where the ceiling is to be imposed, it is apparent that over a period of one human generation science will suffer a loss of its traditional exponential growth and approach the critical point marking its senile limit.

However, growths that have long been exponential seem not to relish the idea of being flattened. Before they reach a midpoint they begin to twist and turn, and, like impish spirits, change their shapes and definitions so as not to be exterminated against that terrible ceiling (Fig. 7). Or, in less anthropomorphic terms, the cybernetic phenomenon of hunting sets in and the curve begins to oscillate wildly. The newly felt constriction produces restorative reaction, but the restored growth first wildly overshoots the mark and then plunges to greater depths than before. If the reaction is successful, its value usually seems to lie in so transforming what is being measured that it takes a new lease on life and rises with a new vigor until, at last, it must meet its doom.

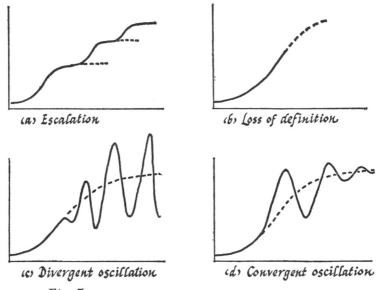

(a) Escalation

(b) Loss of definition

(c) Divergent oscillation

(d) Convergent oscillation

Fig. 7. WAYS IN WHICH LOGISTIC GROWTH MAY
REACT TO CEILING CONDITIONS

In escalation, new logistics are born as the old ones die, in loss of definition it becomes impossible to continue to measure the variable in the same way or in the same units, and in oscillation (convergent and divergent) cybernetic forces attempt to restore free growth.

One therefore finds two variants of the traditional logistic curve that are more frequent than the plain S-shaped ogive. In both cases the variant sets in some time during the inflection, presumably at a time when the privations of the loss of exponential growth become unbearable. If a slight change of definition of the thing that is being measured can be so allowed as to count a new phenomenon on equal terms with the old, the new logistic curve rises phoenixlike on the ashes of the old, a phenomenon first adequately recognized by Holton and felicitously called by him "escalation." Alternatively, if the changed conditions do not admit a new exponential growth, there will be violent fluctuations persisting until the statistic becomes so ill-defined as to be uncountable, or in some cases the fluctuations decline logarithmically to a stable maximum. At times death may even follow this attainment of maturity, so that instead of a stable maximum there is a slow decline back to zero, or a sudden change of definition making it impossible to measure the index and terminating the curve abruptly in midair.

Logistic curves such as these have become well known in numerous analyses of historical time-series, especially those concerning the growth of science and technology. The plain curve is well illustrated in the birth and death of railroad track mileage; in this case the maximum is followed by an eventual decline as tracks are torn up and lines closed down. The curve followed by hunting fluctuations appears in the figures for the production of such technological raw materials as coal and metals (Fig. 8).[6] The escalated curves are probably the most common and can be seen in the number of universities founded; the separate steps here beautifully reflect the different tradi-

[6] S. G. Lasky, "Mineral industry futures can be predicted," *Engineering and Mining Journal,* 152 (August, 1951), 60; 156 (September, 1955), 94.

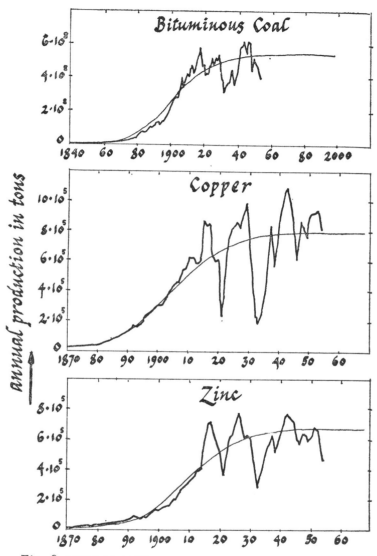

Fig. 8. LOGISTIC GROWTH OF RAW MATERIAL PRODUCTION, SHOWING OSCILLATION ON ATTAINING CEILING CONDITIONS

Adapted from S. G. Lasky, "Mineral industry futures can be predicted," *Engineering and Mining Journal,* 156 (September, 1955).

tions of the medieval universities and the Renaissance foundations (Fig. 9).

They can be seen again in the now-familiar graph, first presented humorously by Fermi,[7] showing the power of acceler-

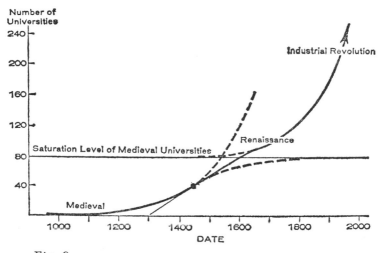

Fig. 9. NUMBER OF UNIVERSITIES FOUNDED IN EUROPE

From the foundation at Cairo in 950 up to ca. 1460 there is pure exponential growth, doubling in about 100 years. Thereafter saturation sets in, so that the midregion of the sigmoid extends from 1300 to ca. 1610. Between 1460 and 1610 is a period of transition to the new form of universities, a growth that also proceeds exponentially as if it had started from unity ca. 1450 and doubling every 66 years. There is probably an ever-greater transition to yet faster growth starting at the end of the Industrial Revolution. From Derek J. de Solla Price, *Science Since Babylon* (New Haven, Yale University Press, 1961).

[7] The exponential growth of accelerators was first noted by John P. Blewett in an Internal Report of the Cosmotron Department of Brookhaven National Laboratory, written on June 9, 1950. The first public presentation of this material was made by Fermi in his address as retiring President, at the American Physical Society meeting in January, 1954. Figure 10 is a later version from M. S. Livingston and J. P. Blewett, *Particle Accelerators* (New York, McGraw-Hill Book Company, Inc., 1962), p. 6.

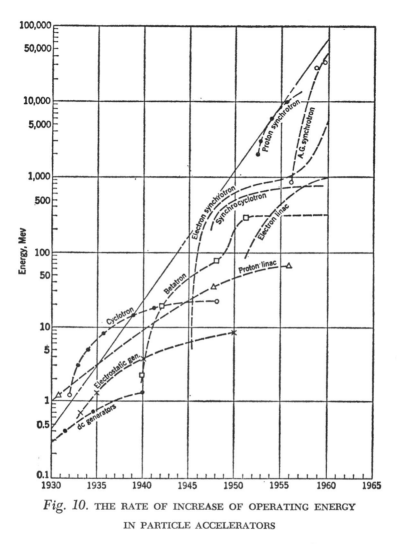

Fig. 10. THE RATE OF INCREASE OF OPERATING ENERGY
IN PARTICLE ACCELERATORS

From M. S. Livingston and J. P. Blewett, *Particle Accelerators* (New
York, McGraw-Hill Book Company, Inc., 1962), p. 6, Fig. 1.1, used by
permission.

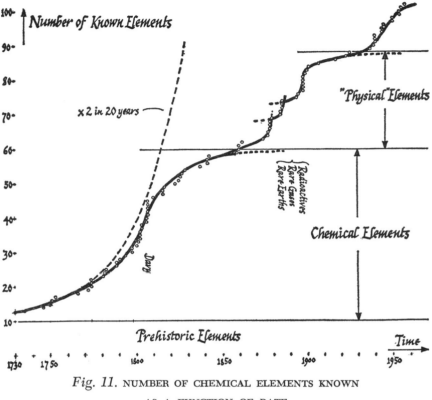

Fig. 11. NUMBER OF CHEMICAL ELEMENTS KNOWN
AS A FUNCTION OF DATE

After the work of Davy there is a clear logistic decline followed by a set of escalations corresponding to the discovery of elements by techniques that are predominantly physical. Around 1950 is the latest escalation produced by the manufacture of trans-uranic elements.

ators (Fig. 10). It becomes less and less humorous as it goes on faithfully predicting when yet another major advance in method is needed to produce another step in the escalation. Yet, again, escalations can be seen in the curve showing the number of chemical elements known as a function of date (Fig. 11). Omitting the first ten, which were known to prehistoric man, we have a steady exponential growth, doubling a shade more rapidly than every 20 years, followed by a midpoint in about 1807 when Sir Humphrey Davy had his heyday, then a period of decline when the first 60 elements had been found. By the end of the nineteenth century, when new methods, physical rather than chemical, led to new classes of elements, there appeared a new bunch of ogives, then a halt until the big machines enabled man to create the last batch of highly unstable and short-lived trans-uranic elements.

From this we are led to suggest a second basic law of the analysis of science: all the apparently exponential laws of growth must ultimately be logistic, and this implies a period of crisis extending on either side of the date of midpoint for about a generation. The outcome of the battle at the point of no return is complete reorganization or violent fluctuation or death of the variable.

Now that we know something about the pathological after-life of a logistic curve, and that such things occur in practice in several special branches of science and technology, let us re-open the question of the growth curve of science as a whole. We have seen that it has had an extraordinarily long life of purely exponential growth and that at some time this must begin to break down and be followed by a generation-long interval of increasing restraint which may tauten its sinews for a jump either toward escalation or toward violent fluctuation. The detailed nature of this change, and any interpretation of it, must depend on what we are measuring and on how such an index is compiled.

Even without such definition and analysis one can immediately deduce various characteristics of such a period. Clearly there will be rapidly increasing concern over those problems of manpower, literature, and expenditure, that demand solution by reorganization. Further, such changes as are successful will lead to a fresh escalation of rapid adaptation and growth. Changes not efficient or radical enough to cause such an off-shoot will lead to a hunting, producing violent fluctuations that will perhaps smooth out at last.

Such an analysis seems to imply that the state called Big Science actually marks the onset of those new conditions that will break the tradition of centuries and give rise to new escalations, violent huntings, redefinitions of our basic terms, and all the other phenomena associated with the upper limit. I will suggest that at some time, undetermined as yet but probably during the 1940s or 1950s, we passed through the midperiod in general logistic growth of science's body politic.

Thus, although we recognize from our discussion so far that saturation is ultimately inevitable, it is far too approximate to indicate when and in what circumstances saturation will begin. We now maintain that it may already have arrived. It may seem odd to suggest this when we have used only a few percent of the manpower and money of the country, but in the next chapter it will appear that this few percent actually represents an approach to saturation and an exhausting of our resources that nearly (within a factor of two) scrapes the bottom of the barrel.

At all events, the appearance of new phenomena in the involvement of science with society seems to indicate something radically different from the steady growth characteristic of the entire historic past. The new era shows all the familiar syndromes of saturation. This, I must add, is a counsel of hope rather than despair. Saturation seldom implies death, but rather that we have the beginning of new and exciting tactics for science, operating with quite new ground rules.

It is, however, a grave business, for Big Science interpreted thus becomes an uncomfortably brief interlude between the traditional centuries of Little Science and the impending period following transition. If we expect to discourse in scientific style about science, and to plan accordingly, we shall have to call this approaching period New Science, or Stable Saturation; if we have no such hopes, we must call it senility.

(2)

GALTON
REVISITED

FRANCIS GALTON (1822–1911), grandson of Erasmus Darwin, was one of the most versatile and curious minds of the nineteenth century. He brought fingerprinting to Scotland Yard, founded the Eugenic Society which advocated breeding of the human race on rational principles, and, above all, gave a flying start to the science of mathematical genetics. His passion was to count everything and reduce it to statistics. Those who see the social sciences rising on a solid foundation of quantified measurements and mathematical theory might well take him as a patron saint rather than Sir William Petty, who is usually seen as the first to bring numbers into the study of people by analyzing the bills of mortality in the seventeenth century.

Galton's passion shows itself best, I feel, in two essays that may seem more frivolous to us than they did to him. In the first, he computed the additional years of life enjoyed by the Royal Family and the clergy because of the prayers offered up for them by the greater part of the population; the result was a negative number. In the second, to relieve the tedium of sitting for a portrait painter, on two different occasions he computed the number of brush strokes and found about 20,000 to the portrait;

just the same number, he calculated, as the hand movements that went into the knitting of a pair of socks.[1]

Let it not be thought that Galton was some sort of crank. His serious work was of the highest standards of scholarship and importance, but he is now increasingly neglected because, although his researches were founded on the exciting and valid basis of Darwin's theory of evolution, Galton had missed the true mechanism of genetic action, discovered by his exact contemporary, Mendel. Mendel published his findings just five years before Galton's book on hereditary genius,[2] but was not discovered by the outside world until Galton was nearly 80.

We shall examine his book *Hereditary Genius,* and, with particular attention, his special study, *English Men of Science* (London, 1874). In these works Galton is primarily concerned with his thesis that great men, including creative scientists, tend to be related and that therefore a series of elite families contributed perhaps the majority of distinguished statesmen, scientists, poets, judges, and military commanders, of his day and of the past. His main work is full of pitfalls, and currently we are not concerned so much with the Galtonian approach to genetics as we are with several of his interesting side investigations. These are his pioneer studies of the distribution of quality among distinguished scientists, and a set of summaries that we should nowadays call sociological and psychological, telling us something about the characteristics of these exceptional men.

We intend to review these two main lines in the light of the twentieth century and its extensions of Galton's work. The first,

---

[1] Karl Pearson, *The Life, Letters and Labours of Francis Galton* (New York, Cambridge University Press, 1914–30), see especially Vol. IIIa, p. 125.

[2] Francis Galton, *Hereditary Genius* (London, 1869; reprinted by Meridian Books, 1962).

telling us how many men or scientific papers or pieces of research there are at each of several levels of quality, is necessary if we are to understand the nature of scientific quality, and this knowledge is a prerequisite to the interpretation of the several different index measures previously mentioned in connection with the basic laws governing the exponential and logistic rates of growth of science. The second will help us formulate ground rules for what to expect of scientists when the change of conditions produced by Big Science or Saturation Science alters their circumstances from those they had known in past ages.

Galton began by estimating how rare in the England of his day were various types of men who were engaged in human affairs generally and in science particularly and who were of sundry degrees of eminence. Using the criterion that a man was eminent if his name appeared in a short biographical compilation of 2500 *Men of the Time* that had just been published, or in the select columns of obituary notices in *The Times*, he found that such noteworthiness had an incidence of about one person for every 2000 adult males or one person in 20,000 of the general population—a mere handful alive at any time in the country.

For eminent scientists he set a standard which demanded that they should be not merely Fellows of the Royal Society—a meaningful honor since the reforms of election under Mr. Justice Groves some 30 years before—but that they must be further distinguished by a university chair; by a medal presented by a learned society, or an office held in such a body; or by membership in some elite scientific club of academic worth. His count of people from whom he could obtain the full biographical information desired was 180, and he estimated that in the entire country there might be at the most 300 such people.

Reckoning that half of them were between the ages of 50

and 65, he calculated that the chance of rising to such stature was about 1 in 10,000 adult males of this age group, a figure roughly corresponding to 1 in 100,000 of the general population. However, since the general biographical lists show that only about 1 in 10 eminent men was engaged in science or medicine, then by his previous standards there should only have been about one eminent scientist for every 200,000 of the general population. The fact that Galton supposes there to have been twice as many, means either that he was erring on the side of generosity in estimating the numbers of good scientists who should have been on his list and were not, or that the tendency is to cast a broader net when looking for great scientists than when looking for great men in general.

The utility of this investigation is that it provides an estimate of the number of scientific persons whom Galton considered important enough to be well worth discussion, but without limiting the scope to include such a small group that it would leave the investigator generalizing about a mere handful of geniuses. Thus, between 5 and 10 persons in a million fall within this category. How does this compare with the state of affairs since Galton's time?

Fortunately there is an admirable biographical compilation, *American Men of Science*, that has run through 10 editions between 1903 and 1960. The editor, J. McKeen Cattell (himself a prominent psychologist), rendered signal service by starring the most noteworthy names, beginning with an original 1000 and adding to this number as each new edition appeared.[3] It so happens that in the first edition there are about 11 starred

---

[3] Here and later we have made considerable use of the extensive analysis in S. S. Visher, *Scientists Starred 1903–1943 in "American Men of Science,"* (Baltimore, The Johns Hopkins Press, 1947).

names to a million population of the United States, in the volume for 1938 there are about 12.4 to a million, and that both figures are of the same order of magnitude as that found by Galton. Certainly there appears to have been no vast change in the number of "eminent" men of science to a million population, either on moving our scene of inquiry from Britain to the United States or on following it through nearly a doubling of the United States population. One may argue that Galton's standard of distinction is not the same as Cattell's. One may maintain with even greater reason that Cattell's arbitrary allocation of a set quota of 1000 stars originally, with a fixed increment thereafter, was perhaps out of all proportion to a constant standard of eminence. In spite of this, we can find no rapid changes in this estimated incidence of scientific eminence.

If in studying *American Men of Science* we look not at the starred names alone but at all of them, we observe a most striking change in order of magnitude with the passing of time (Table 1). Just to run one's eye along the set of 10 editions on a shelf is to feel an immediate respect for the power of exponential growth.

It is apparent that within the past 50 years there has been a sixteenfold increase in the number of men, an exponential growth with a doubling period of about 12½ years, a figure already suggested as typifying the growth of science. Even in relation to the size of the general population it can be seen that the same half-century has multiplied the density of scientists by a factor of eight, a doubling in about 17 years. Another four such half-centuries of regular growth would give us more than two million American men of science per million population, if it were not that exponential growths inevitably become logistic and die.

We have already shown that because of this logistic machinery the prospect for the immediate future is more interesting than that of a slow death from suffocation in A.D. 2160. Our crisis seems to be but a few decades ahead, and far more involved with the nature of the growth than with the final exhaustion of the population. It is therefore a matter of some interest to seek the reason why, in spite of this general rapid

TABLE 1

NUMBER OF MEN CITED IN EDITIONS OF
AMERICAN MEN OF SCIENCE

Year of publication	Number of men	Number/million population U.S.
1903	4,000	50
1910	5,500	60
1921	9,500	90
1928	13,500	110
1933	22,000	175
1938	28,000	220
1944	34,000	240
1948	50,000	340
1955	74,000	440
1960 (omitting social sciences)	96,000	480

exponential growth of scientific manpower—and, incidentally, of its publications and budgets—the number of truly great men does not seem to change with the same quick exuberance.

The root of the trouble, as Galton well perceived, lies in the establishment of any objective standard of eminence not dependent upon time. Conceivably, all that we have said is that when men are chosen by degrees of selectivity that run to orders of 10 in a million they become remarkable to this standard extent. The same problem is encountered in most recent evaluations of the high-talent population on the basis of intelligence tests. For example, one may say that on an AGCT (Army General Classification Test) type of test only one man in 10,000 of his age group might score more than 170, one in 100,000 more than 180, one in 1,000,000 more than 190, and so on, with an order of magnitude for each 10 (more accurately, 11) points that raise the stakes. But one cannot usefully say that eminence begins at a score of 172 and not below. Even if genius were merely a matter of the talents being measured by the test in hand, there would be no clear cutoff, only a gradual falling off of the population as the standards are raised. The fault lies not so much in the definition of what constitutes scientific ability as in the false premise that distinction or genius can be decided on a yes-or-no-basis.

Results more accurate, although not much more, can be achieved by taking a reasonably small group of tabulated men, discoveries, or even scientific institutions, journals, and countries, and carefully marking in some special way those that were distinguished. For eminent men, for example, one might use as criteria selection to give invited papers, and to receive medals and other awards, such as Nobel Prizes. This gives the usual sort of exponential growth, but with a doubling time considerably longer than 10 years. For example, in a select, apparently superior group of modern scientists in any large field, drawn from standard biographical handbooks or other sources that select only a small elite, the doubling time is about 20 years. One obtains about the same figure for any list of selected great scientific discoveries.

To improve the strength and significance of this result, it is clearly necessary to make some statement about degrees of eminence that would give not a dichotomy of distinguished and undistinguished but rather a sliding scale, a sort of velocity distribution. One such scale—the traditional one used by deans and other employers as a measure of scientific success—is the number of publications produced by each man in accepted scientific journals. Let it be freely admitted at the outset that this is a bad scale. Who dares to balance one paper of Einstein on relativity against even a hundred papers by John Doe, Ph.D., on the elastic constant of the various timbers (one to a paper) of the forests of Lower Basutoland?

The scale is bad if for no other reason than that its existence has moved people to publish merely because this is how they may be judged. Nevertheless, it makes a starting point, and later on it may be refined to meet objections. We shall show, for example, that all such distributions are of the same type and, thus, though one cannot directly measure "scientific ability," one may reasonably deduce properties of its presumed distribution. We shall also have to enter the caveat that the scale may not be directly applicable to the era of Big Science, which has involved so much collaborative work that one cannot easily determine a man's score. This is another point to be reserved for later elaboration.

Let us not begin with too pessimistic an outlook on the worth of this investigation. Flagrant violations there may be, but on the whole there is, whether we like it or not, a reasonably good correlation between the eminence of a scientist and his productivity of papers. It takes persistence and perseverance to be a good scientist, and these are frequently reflected in a sustained production of scholarly writing. Then, again, it may be well demonstrated that the list of high scorers contains a large proportion of names that are not only well known but even honored. Conversely, the low-scoring end of the list contains fewer such names in terms of absolute numbers, and much fewer in proportion.

Exactly such a study was made by Wayne Dennis. Using as his source the National Academy of Sciences *Biographical Memoirs* for 1943–52, he showed that of the 41 men who died after a full life, having reached the age of 70, the top man had 768 publications, the bottom 27. The average number of publications was more than 200, and only 15 persons had fewer than 100 in their bibliographies. Similarly, a list of 25 eminent nineteenth-century scientists showed that all but one were in the range of 61 to 307 items.[4] Further, taking a sample from the *Royal Society Bibliography of Scientific Literature 1800–1900*, he showed that the most productive 10 percent of all authors, having each more than 50 publications, were of such caliber that 50 percent of them gained the distinction of mention in the *Encyclopaedia Britannica;* of the top 5 percent, each of whom had more than 140 items to his bibliography, some 70 percent received such mention. None of those mentioned in the *Encyclopaedia* by virtue of their scientific work had fewer than seven publications.

Thus, although there is no guarantee that the small producer is a nonentity and the big producer a distinguished scientist, or even that the order of merit follows the order of productivity, there is a strong correlation,[5] and we are interested in looking deeper into the relative distribution of big- and small-output writers of scientific literature. Such studies are easy to make by counting the number of items under each author's name in

[4] The exception being Riemann, who published only 19 papers but died at the age of 40.

[5] Productivity is therefore one of many factors.

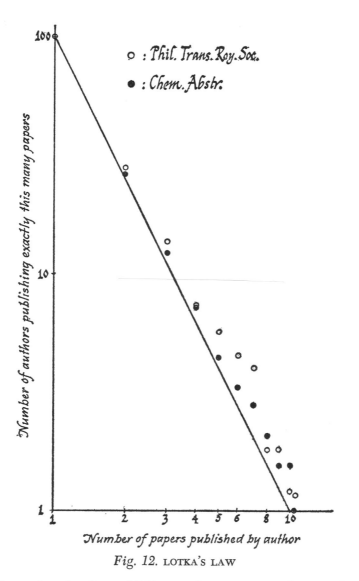

Fig. 12. LOTKA'S LAW

The number of authors publishing exactly *n* papers, as a function of *n*.
The open circles represent data taken from the first index volume of the
abridged *Philosophical Transactions of the Royal Society of London*
(17th and early 18th centuries), the filled circles those from the 1907–16
decennial index of *Chemical Abstracts*. The straight line shows the exact
inverse-square law of Lotka. All data are reduced to a basis of exactly
100 authors publishing but a single paper.

the cumulative index of a journal. A pioneer investigation of this sort was made by Lotka,[6] and several others have since repeated such head counts. They all confirm a simple, basic result that does not seem to depend upon the type of science or the date of the index volume; the only requirement is that the index extend over a number of years sufficient to enable those who can produce more than a couple of papers to do so.

The result of this investigation is an inverse-square law of productivity (Fig. 12). The number of people producing n papers is proportional to $1/n^2$. For every 100 authors who produce but a single paper in a certain period, there are 25 with two, 11 with three, and so on. Putting it a little differently by permitting the results to cumulate, one achieves an integration that gives approximately an inverse first-power law for the number of people who produce more than n papers; thus, about one in five authors produces five papers or more, and one in ten produces at least ten papers (Fig. 13).

It is surprising that such a simple law should be followed so accurately and that one should find the same distribution of scientific productivity in the early volumes of the Royal Society as in data from the twentieth-century *Chemical Abstracts*. The regularity, I suggest, tells us something about the nature of the scores we are keeping. An inverse-square law probability distribution, or an inverse first power for the cumulative probability, is nothing like either the normal Gaussian or Poisson distributions, or any of the other such curves given by normal linear measure of events that go by chance. If the number of scientific papers were distributed in a manner similar to that of

[6] Alfred J. Lotka, "The frequency distribution of scientific productivity," *Journal of the Washington Academy of Sciences*, 16 (1926), 317. For a fuller analysis and justification see Herbert A. Simon, *Models of Man, Social and National* (New York, John Wiley and Sons, Inc., 1957), p. 160.

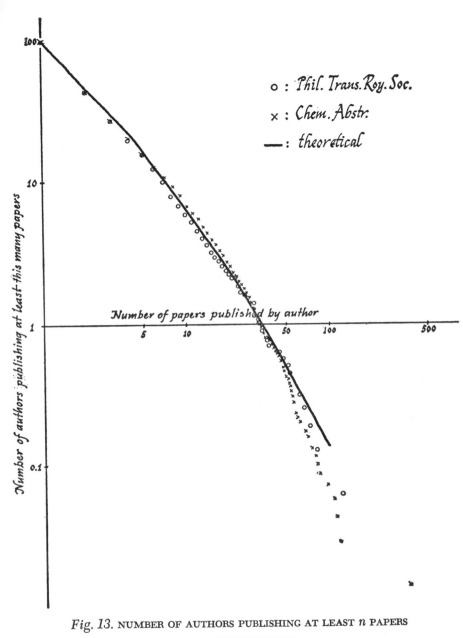

Fig. 13. NUMBER OF AUTHORS PUBLISHING AT LEAST n PAPERS
AS A FUNCTION OF n

Same data, and same reduction as for Fig. 12, but full curve here is modified to a form that takes account of Lotka's overestimation of the number of highly prolific authors (see footnote 8, Chapter 2).

the number of men with various heights, or the number kicked to death by horses, we should find far fewer large scores. Scientific papers do not rain from heaven so that they are distributed by chance; on the contrary, up to a point, the more you

TABLE 2

SCHEMATIC TABLE SHOWING NUMBERS OF AUTHORS
OF VARIOUS DEGREES OF PRODUCTIVITY (IN
PAPERS PER LIFETIME) AND NUMBERS
OF PAPERS SO PRODUCED [a]

Papers/man	Men	Papers	
1	100	100	(The 75 percent of men who
2	25	50	are low scorers produce one-
3	11.1	33.3	quarter of all papers.)
4	6.2	25	
5	4	20	
6	2.8	16.7	
7	2	14.2	
8	1.5	12.5	
9	1.2	11.1	
10	1	10	
10–11.1	1	10+	
11.1–12.5	1	11.1+	
12.5–14.2	1	12.5+	
14.2–16.7	1	14.2+	(Subtotal: 10 men produce
16.7–20	1	16.7+	more than 50 percent of all
20–25	1	20+	papers.)
25–33.3	1	25+	
33.3–50	1	33.3+	
50–100	1	50+	(The top two men produce
Over 100	1	100+	one-quarter of all papers.)
Total	165	586+	

Average papers/man = 586/165 = 3.54

[a] Table constructed on basis of exactly 100 men with a single published paper. Other entries computed from Lotka's law.

have the easier it seems to be to get the next, a principle to which we shall return later.

Let us first examine the nature of the crude inverse-square law of productivity (Table 3). If one computes the total production of those who write n papers, it emerges that the large number of low producers account for about as much of the total as the small number of large producers; in a simple schematic case, symmetry may be shown to a point corresponding to the square root of the total number of men, or the score of the highest producer. If there are 100 authors, and the most prolific has a score of 100 papers, half of all the papers will have been written by the 10 highest scorers, and the other half by those with fewer than 10 papers each. In fact, in this ideal case, a full quarter of the papers have been written by the top two men, and another quarter by those who publish only one or two items.

This immediately gives an objective method for separating the major from the minor contributors. One may set a limit and say that half the work is done by those with more than 10 papers to their credit, or that the number of high producers seems to be the same order of magnitude as the square root of the total number of authors. The first way, setting some quota of 10 or so papers, which may be termed "Deans' method," is familiar enough; the second way, suggesting that the number of men goes up as the square of the number of good ones, seems consistent with the previous findings that the number of scientists doubles every 10 years, but the number of noteworthy scientists only every 20 years.

Unfortunately, Lotka's simple inverse-square law needs modification in the case of high scorers (Fig. 14). Beyond the division lines mentioned, the number of people falls off more

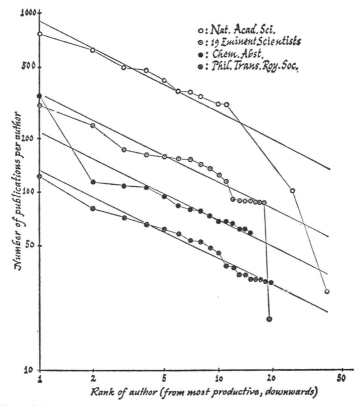

Fig. 14. NUMBERS OF PUBLICATIONS OF FOUR SERIES OF HIGHLY
DISTINGUISHED AND (INCIDENTALLY) HIGHLY PROLIFIC
AUTHORS, EACH RANKED WITHIN THE SERIES

The series are (1) members of the National Academy of Sciences, drawn
from obituary bibliographies, (2) nineteen eminent scientists of the 19th
century, (3) most prolific authors in decennial index of *Chemical Abstracts*, (4) index to Vols. 1–70, *Philosophical Transactions of the Royal
Society.*

rapidly than the inverse square, more nearly approximating the inverse cube. It amounts to the same thing to say that their *cumulative* number falls off as the square of the score rather than as its first power. The data from the work of Lotka and Dennis [7] agree completely on this, i.e., if one ranks the high scorers in order of merit, their scores fall as the square root of the ranks in all cases.

By means of this one may easily derive a law which holds both for the low and high scorers and which slightly cuts down the upper tail of the Lotka distribution.[8] One can see that this should be qualitatively necessary, since otherwise the maximum scores of published papers in a lifetime would be thousands and even tens of thousands rather than the several hundreds that seem to represent even the most prolific scientific

[7] Wayne Dennis, "Bibliographies of eminent scientists," *The Scientific Monthly*, 79 (September, 1954), 180–83.

[8] For the graphical presentations given here we have used a distribution law of the form

$$N = k \left(\frac{1}{p} - \frac{1}{a+p} \right) = \frac{ak}{p(a+p)},$$

where N is the cumulative number of men who publish at least p scientific papers within a given interval of time (here taken as a lifetime). For those of low productivity $1 < p < a$, and the law tends to the inverse first-power form $N = k/p$, while for the high-productivity authors we have $a < p < \infty$, and the law approximates the inverse-square form $N = ak/p^2$. We find that the available data may be fitted by taking the boundary between high and low productivities at $a = 15$ papers per lifetime.

From the given distribution law one is able to compute in sequence the number of people publishing exactly p papers, the number of papers published in all by such people and, finally, the cumulative number of papers published by the cumulative number of authors. This enables one to calculate all the properties of such a distribution in terms of the parameter, a, and the arbitrary constant of proportionality, k. It happens, for example, that the average number of papers per author is given by $1 + (1 + 1/a) \log (1 + a)$ which is very insensitive to the magnitude of a, assuming a value of 3 for $a = 7$, and a value of 4 for $a = 22$.

lives. Cayley, one of the great British mathematicians of the nineteenth century, has 995 items in his collected works—a paper every two to three weeks—and I have failed to find anyone who outstrips this.

This modified law leads to the result that about one-third of the literature and less than one-tenth of the men are associated with high scores. It leads, furthermore, to an average of $3\frac{1}{2}$ papers per man. Thus, if we know how many papers are published in a field, we can compute the number of men who have written them, even the much smaller number who must be reckoned as distinguished contributors to that field. Thus, for a field containing 1000 papers, there will be about 300 authors. About 180 of them will not get beyond their first paper, but another 30 will be above our cutoff of 10 papers each, and 10 will be highly prolific, major contributors.

More important than numerical information is the proved existence of a workable distribution law. One may make an interesting comparison between this and the famous Pareto law of distribution of income.[9] Instead of a form following $1/n$ for small values and $1/n^2$ for large, Pareto found that cumulative figures for income followed, almost exactly, and constantly over a long time in different countries, a law of $1/n^{1.5}$—just midway between our two forms. Why is there such an empirical law, and why is it so very different from the usual laws of errors, horse kicks, and other probability distributions?

The reason lies, I think, in the simple fact that the number of publications is not a linear additive measure of productivity in the way required for Gaussian distributions. Our cutoff point is not the average of the highest score and the lowest but rather their geometric mean. One feels intuitively that the step from

[9] The law was proposed in detail in V. Pareto, *Cours d'économie politique* (1897), Vol. 2, pp. 299–345.

three papers to six is similar to that from 30 to 60 rather than that from 30 to 33. Because of all this it is reasonable to suggest that we have here something like the approximate law of Fechner or Weber in experimental psychology, wherein the true measure of the response is taken not by the magnitude of the stimulus but by its logarithm; we must have equal intervals of effort corresponding to equal ratios of numbers of publications.[10]

We may define a man's solidness, s (how solid a fellow is he?) as the logarithm of his life's score of papers. The logarithm of the number of men having at least s units of solidness of productivity will at first fall linearly with s, then more rapidly as it approaches the fixed upper limit of 1000 papers, beyond which no man has achieved. In other words, for every unit increase in solidness, the number of men attaining such solidness is cut by some almost constant factor. Now this fall of the population by a constant factor for each unit increase of s is exactly what one finds in the tail of a normal probability distribution. For example, if we take the standard AGCT intelligence-test distribution, which is so arranged that the norm is 100 on the scale, with half the population above and half below, and a spread such that the quartiles are at 80 and 120 (i.e., the standard deviation is 20), then for scores over about 140 (and also less than 60) the number of cases in the tail drops by a factor of 10 for every 10 points on the scale. If we measure solidness by

[10] Cf. Galton's citation of the marks gained by the wranglers in the Cambridge Mathematical Tripos. Their scores, as nearly as possible on an objective open scale of merit, were such that the top candidate in each year got almost twice the marks of the second, and 30 times that of the 100th candidate.

The log-normal character of scientific productivity distributions has previously been suggested by William Shockley, "On the statistics of individual variations of productivity in research laboratories," *Proceedings of the Institute of Radio Engineers,* 45 (1957), 279, 1409.

logarithms to base 10, then every unit of s corresponds to about 11 points on the AGCT scale for all but the most solid scientific citizens, and for these it rises to about 20 points.

Pareto's law may therefore be regarded as merely the result of combining a reasonable probability distribution of capabilities with a Fechner's law measure of the effectiveness of these capabilities. In the case of scientific productivity we find a similar happy accounting on a theoretical basis for the shape of the empirical law. The only difference between the distributions of money and papers, or the more generalized distribution found by Zipf to account for nearly all natural distributions of things ranked in order of size, is that for science there is a definite upper limit to the amount that one man can accomplish in a lifetime.

Our one remaining uncertainty about the new law of normal distribution of scientific solidness is that we do not know where to put the beginning of the scale. What AGCT score corresponds to the state $s = 0$, the minimal state of one scientific publication during a lifetime? If, without altering the presumably absolute and objective minimum standards for a scientific paper, one could induce every member of the population to go through the motions of education and professional training, and try to achieve this goal, how many would succeed?

This question is extraordinarily difficult to answer, for apart from a great corpus of general intelligence tests the competence level of the quantitative art is low when applied to deciding what makes for scientific creativity. On the basis of our newly won theory, one can now hazard a guess from intelligence tests alone. The fundamental investigations by Harmon [11] on records

---

[11] Lindsey R. Harmon, "The high school backgrounds of science doctorates," *Science,* 133 (March 10, 1961), 679, also published at length in *Scientific Manpower* 1960 (NSF 61-34, May 1961), pp. 14–28.

of the United States crop of Ph.D.'s for 1958 enable us to say something of the incidence and of the intelligence-test characteristics of this group. Now, the Ph.D. and the editorial standards of learned periodical publications are things that we have done our best to keep constant. It is therefore reasonable to identify the minimum effort of writing a single scientific paper with that demanded by the "sheepskin gateway" to the road of research. Although it is agreed that these things do not coincide, since some Ph.D.'s never publish even their theses, whereas many authors are not doctors, yet at worst they should differ by some reasonably constant ratio not too far from unity.

Harmon found that in an age group of the population numbering about 2,400,000 there arises an annual crop of about 8000 Ph.D.'s in all fields, the physical and biological sciences together comprising about half the total. As one might expect, the intelligence-test scores for this group were considerably higher than the general level, the average being AGCT 130·8 for the mode of the distribution. Taken by fields, there was a variation from 140·3 for physics to 123·3 for Ph.D.'s in education:

Physics	140·3
Mathematics	138·2
Engineering	134·8
Geology	133·3
Arts and humanities	132·1
Social sciences	132·0
Natural sciences	131·7
Chemistry	131·5
Biology	126·1
Education	123·3

When these data were applied to the general population in the same age group, it appeared that at the highest level of intelligence recorded, AGCT 170+, about one person in five received a Ph.D., although the general incidence of doctorates in the age group was only 1 in 3000. Thus, intelligence has a lot to do with the gaining of Ph.D.'s. If we now consider it plausible that this current figure of one in five refers to those superior beings who become highly productive scientists, one could contemplate using all means, fair and foul, to close the gap so that they would all earn Ph.D.'s or even scientific Ph.D.'s.

We know now that the total number of scientists goes up as the square, more or less, of the number of good ones. Therefore, if we want to multiply the good scientists by five, we must multiply the whole group by 25. Instead of an age group of about 8000 Ph.D.'s in mixed subjects, we should then have about 200,000, all in science. As it happens, the intelligence distribution shows that in an age group of 2,400,000, a few more than 160,000 achieve AGCT 130, and so we have a minimal cutoff for possible scientists that is only slightly less than the present mode found for Ph.D.'s, both scientific and otherwise. The two methods thus coincide to indicate that about 6 to 8 percent of the population at most could be minimal scientists.

Apparently, then, the scale of solidness in scientific publication should have its zero placed at an AGCT level of about 130, corresponding to about one person in every 15 in an age group. Attractive though it may be to perceive such a cutoff point, agreeing as it does so well with the present norm for Ph.D.'s, the implications are grave. At first sight it appears that at present we are tapping only about one in 25 of those who could become scientists at all, and a fifth of those who would be outstanding scientists. If we took all the talent of the population with no loss or wastage, we should then have 8,000,000 scientists writing papers in the United States,[12] and, of these, 80,000 would be highly productive, with more than 10 papers each. Thus, we should have a roll of 40,000 scientists to a million population, and, of these, 400 in a million would be men of note. Galton, you remember, found about 5 to 10 eminent scientists in a million population, and the early volumes of *American Men of Science* showed 50 in a million. Thus, in the density of good scientists we have left one more order of magnitude at the most and, even at the expense of all other high-talent occupations, science is not likely to engross more than 8 percent of the population. Even so, it looks as if the decreasing return of good scientists to every 100 Ph.D.'s will make it more and more difficult to reach a level of this magnitude. Just how strong is this limitation? Is it possible that the level of good scientists cannot rise by the factor of five that we have presumed?

Almost half of the factor is accounted for by the wastage of scientific womanpower, a wastage that the U.S.S.R. has partially checked but that we seem unable to avoid. Another factor of two might be attributed to the lack of opportunity and incentive in regions outside the big cities where schools are good and competition and inspiration keen. Indeed, all things considered, the high proportion of talented manpower successfully diverted into science at present is surely to our credit. But if the level cannot indeed rise, then we are, as we have already conjectured, about halfway toward saturation at the top end of the scale, and any increase in numbers of scientists must produce an even greater preponderance of manpower able to write scientific papers, but not able to write distinguished ones. It gives serious pause to thoughts about the future of scientific education. Is it worth much sacrifice?

[12] This is more than twice the present *world* population of scientists.

I think we have now laid the theoretical basis for this study of science. It is remarkably similar to the study of econometrics. On the one hand we have the dynamic treatment that gives us time series, first of exponential growth, then of the saturated growth resulting in standard logistic curves. On the other hand, we have the statics of a distribution law similar to that of Pareto. The extent of the difference between analyzing science and analyzing business lies in the parameters. The main exponential part of the growth of science doubles in 10 years only, which is much more rapid than all else; the characteristic index of the distribution law is one at the low end and two at the high, instead of a uniform 1·5.

The additional contributions that we have made lie in providing a reasonable theoretical basis for our Pareto law and in showing that, although the average number of papers per author remains sensibly constant, one may make a split between those whose productivity is high and that much larger mass of authors whose productivity is low. This mass is seen to grow as the square of the number of high scorers, and therefore the number of high scorers will appear to double only every 20 years.

The Fechner law principle which we invoked to reduce the Pareto-like distribution to the sort of linear and additive measure that is necessary for a standard probability curve is much more powerful than we have yet assumed. If we may take in general the solidness of a body of publications as measured by the logarithm of the number of papers, it has further interesting consequences. Consider the law of exponential growth previously mentioned as a universal condition of freely expanding science. Obviously, the solidness of the field, the logarithm of the number of papers, grows linearly with time. Thus, since it takes about 50 years for the number of men or number of papers in a field to multiply by 10, there is a unit increase of solidness every half-century.[13]

I cannot quite see why it is so, or how one might judge it other than by pure intuition, but the two units of solidness separating the man who can publish no more than one paper in a lifetime from the one who can write a hundred such papers are essentially the same as those that separate the two states of a subject at dates a century apart. In rough, and misleading, terms one might say that the eminent scientist is a century ahead of the minimal one.

What further implications are there of the assumption that one can measure the progress of a field by the linear march of its solidness? Are such degrees of solidness truly additive? Must we judge one field of a hundred workers adding two units of solidness within a certain time as inferior to 10 separate fields of 10 workers, each of whom will add one unit to each field, making a total of 10 units within the same time?

If such an indication be true, then it seems that science has a strong desire to minimize its solidness rather than make it as large as possible. Beyond the phenomenon of exponential growth, science displays in several ways a tendency to crystallize out, in the sense that big things grow at the expense of the small ones that constitute a sort of mother liquor. Large fields seem to absorb the manpower and subject matter of small ones. Even though new fields, new departments, new institutions, and even new countries arrive on the scientific scene in increasing number, the few previously existing large ones have a nat-

[13] This, then, provides a measure that is linear, not exponential. It is the sort of index which might correspond with Nobel Prizes (which come linearly with time because that is how they are organized); possibly also with unexpected, crucial advances.

ural growth enabling them in general to maintain their lead. It is the exception, rather than the rule, for one of the big blocks to slacken its growth—presumably through the existence of some sort of logistic ceiling that causes it to stagnate—and be overtaken so that it falls in rank.

The fact that the general growth of science increases equally the sizes of the large blocks and the numbers of the small blocks, while presenting an appearance of crystallization, is really not so peculiar. Precisely the same thing happens when the population of a country grows. Instead of being uniformly distributed over the country, it is crystallized out into variously sized blocks called cities. The growth of cities in a country provides a useful model for the growths of scientific blocks within science. As it happens, the hierarchical order of cities or other blocks, ranked by decreasing size, offers yet another example of the same Pareto-like distribution we have already found for the productivity of scientific authors.

In the case of cities, the historical statistics provide a good example of such a distribution on the move, with everything increasing exponentially while maintaining the normal distribution (Fig. 15).[14] Using a plot showing the distribution at each decade, one may see the constant slope of the distribution on a log-log scale and the inexorable march of the intercepts that tell us the magnitude of the biggest city on the one scale and the number of minimal cities (here taken as population 2500) on the other scale. Both increase regularly each decade, taking about 60 years each to go through a power of 10 or, as we have called it before, one unit of solidness. If one looked in detail at

[14] Figure 15 and the following data are from G. K. Zipf, *Human Behavior and the Principle of Least Effort* (Cambridge, Mass., Addison-Wesley Publishing Company, Inc., 1949), p. 420, Fig. 10-2.

the life history of any particular city, its rank would change with time as it outpaced others and was itself outpaced; however, the statistical distribution is remarkably constant.

This general pattern, carrying all the implications of our previous analysis of productivity distribution, is followed fairly

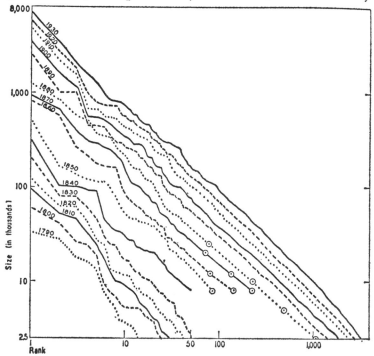

Fig. 15. UNITED STATES, 1790–1930

Communities of 2500 or more inhabitants ranked in the decreasing order of population size. It should be noted that the distribution at any given date shows size decreasing uniformly with rank; as cities become more numerous and all of them increase in size, the distribution pattern is preserved, the curve moving parallel to itself at a constant rate. From George K. Zipf, *Human Behavior and the Principle of Least Effort* (Cambridge, Mass., Addison-Wesley Publishing Company, Inc., 1949), p. 420, Fig. 10-2.

well by such diverse hierarchical lists as those giving the sizes in faculties, or in Ph.D.'s per decade, of the college scientific departments, in any field or in general, in the United States or in the world. It is followed by ranked lists showing the scientific contributions, in terms of papers, journals, or expenditures of the nations of the world, ranging from the few big producers on any scale relative or absolute to the minor production of the large number of underdeveloped countries (Fig. 16).[15]

About this process there is the same sort of essential, built-in *undemocracy* that gives us a nation of cities rather than a country steadily approximating a state of uniform population density. Scientists tend to congregate in fields, in institutions, in countries, and in the use of certain journals. They do not spread out uniformly, however desirable that may or may not be. In particular, the growth is such as to keep relatively constant the balance between the few giants and the mass of pygmies. The number of giants grows so much more slowly than the entire population that there must be more and more pygmies per giant, deploring their own lack of stature and wondering why it is that neither man nor nature pushes us toward egalitarian uniformity.

Value judgments aside, it seems clear that the existence of a reasonable distribution that tells us how many men, papers, countries, or journals there are in each rank of productivity, utility, or whatever you will measure provides a powerful tool. Instead of attempting to get precision in defining which heads to count in exponential growth, one may instead take a crude count and interpret it by means of such a distribution.

Just as one cannot measure the individual velocities of all

[15] Data from a preliminary survey of scientific periodicals by the Library of Congress.

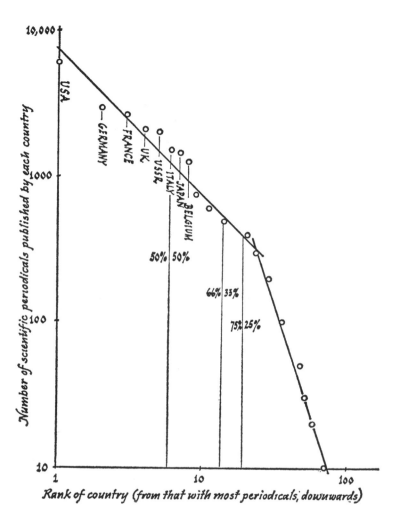

Fig. 16. NUMBER OF SCIENTIFIC PERIODICALS PUBLISHED BY EACH
COUNTRY, RANKED IN DECREASING ORDER OF SUCH NUMBERS

It will be seen that the top six countries account for half of all publications, the top 11 for two-thirds, etc. Productivity of journals falls off
very rapidly for the less prolific countries. Data from a preliminary survey conducted by the Library of Congress.

molecules in a gas, one cannot actually measure the degrees of eminence of all scientists. However, there are reasonable grounds for saying that such measurements, if made, would follow the standard distribution. In particular, we can take this Pareto-like distribution as a hypothesis and see how the consequences agree with gross phenomena which we can measure. We do, in fact, find a reassuring agreement.

Such, then, is the broad mathematical matrix of exponential growth, logistic decay, and distribution functions. It provides us now with a general description of the normal expansion of science and its state at any time. Knowing now the regular behavior, we have a powerful tool for investigating the significant irregularities injected into the system by the gross perturbations of war and revolution, by the logistic birth and death of measurable entities, by genius and crucial discovery, and, in short, by all the organizational changes within the body politic of science and in its relations with the state and society in general.

(3)

INVISIBLE COLLEGES
AND THE AFFLUENT
SCIENTIFIC COMMUTER

FROM ALL the talk of exponential growth and scientific productivity distributions, one might think that scientific papers were produced merely to be counted by deans, administrators, and historians and that the driving force of a scientist should be directed toward producing the maximum number of contributions. This is far from the truth. An almost instinctive reaction away from all this counting nonsense is to agree that each paper represents at least a quantum of useful scientific information and that some single contributions may rise so far above this quantum value that for such a one alone its author would be valued above any random hundred, or even above a hundred more prolific writers.

To take the opposite point of view and look into the tangible results of scientific work more deeply than by mere head-counting, we must know considerably more about the social institutions of science and the psychology of the scientist. The prime object of the scientist is not, after all, the publication of scientific papers. Further, the paper is not for him purely and simply a means of communicating knowledge.

Let us look at the history of the scientific paper. It all began because there were too many books. Here is a cry from the heart of a scholar:

One of the diseases of this age is the multiplicity of books; they doth so overcharge the world that it is not able to digest the abundance of idle matter that is every day hatched and brought forth into the world.

It is chastening to find that these words were written by the rambunctious Barnaby Rich in 1613, half a century before the scientific journal was born. The coming of the learned periodical promised an end to this iniquity of overcharge. Developing in time and spirit together with the newspaper, such publications as the *Philosophical Transactions of the Royal Society* had the stated function of digesting the books and doings of the learned all over Europe. Through them the casual reader might inform himself without the network of personal correspondence, private rumor, and browsing in Europe's bookstores, formerly essential.

At first, however, they did not by any means remit the scholarly obligation to read books and write them. Their original purpose was a social one of finding out what was being done and by whom rather than a scholarly one of publishing new knowledge.[1]

Original publication of short papers by single authors was a distinct innovation in the life of science and, like all innovations, it met with considerable resistance from scientists. Barber [2] has

[1] However, publications of the learned academies as corporate bodies engaged in the experiments and trials for which they had been constituted had appeared before. The *Saggi* of the Accademia del Cimento, which preceded the societies of London and Paris, is a volume of fine research papers published as a complete and final single book, not as a serial.

[2] B. Barber, "Resistance by scientists to scientific discovery," *Scientific Manpower 1960* (National Science Foundation Publication NSF 61-34, May 1961), pp. 36–47.

pointed out that such resistance is part of a vital mechanism of innate conservatism in the body of science. It is a natural counterpart to the open-minded creativity that floods it with too many new ideas, and to the edge of objectivity that forms an eventual means of deciding between true and false.

Such resistance against the new and seemingly illicit practice of publishing papers instead of decent books is seen in the case of Newton. The controversies over his optical papers in the *Philosophical Transactions* were a source of deep distress to him, and afterwards he did not relish publication until it could take the proper form of a finished book, treating the subject from begining to end and meeting all conceivable objections and side arguments. If the journal had been at that time an effective means of communication, we might never have had the *Principia*. Perhaps we should begin to disregard a man's papers and look at his books.

The transformation of the scientific paper into its modern state was not complete until about a century ago. Before that time there was much publication of scientific "snippets," such as the bare mention of something achieved, or a review of observations that had been made and published elsewhere. There were also plenty of monographic publications that would have been books in themselves if only the means for profitable printing and distribution had existed. As late as 1900, some of the most respected journals contained not one scientific paper of the present variety. The difference is not only one of length— if they are too short, they are letters; if too long, monographs.

I would rather make a distinction in the mode of cumulation of the papers. This has to do with the way in which each paper is built on a foundation of previous papers, then in turn is one of several points of departure for the next. The most obvious manifestation of this scholarly bricklaying is the citation of references. One cannot assume that all authors have been accurate, consistent, and conscientious in noting their sources. Some have done too little, others too much. But it is generally evident from a long run of any scientific periodical that around 1850 there appears the familiar modern pattern of explicit reference to previous work on which rests the distinct, well-knit addition that is the ideal burden of each paper. Before that time, though footnoting is as old as scholarship itself—compare the very term *scholia* for the ancient footnote—there is nothing like this attitude toward the accretion of learning.

If, then, the prototype of the modern scientific paper is a social device rather than a technique for cumulating quanta of information, what strong force called it into being and kept it alive? Beyond a doubt, the motive was the establishment and maintenance of intellectual property. It was the need which scientists felt to lay claim to newly won knowledge as their own, the never-gentle art of establishing priority claims.

In a pair of perceptive papers,[3] Robert Merton has analyzed the way in which priority claims and disputes have been omnipresent during the past few centuries of science. The phenomenon emerges as a dominant thread in the history of science, woven through the stories of all men in all lands. It is fair to say that to understand the sociological character of such disputes is more important for the historian than merely to settle such claims.

The evidence makes it plain that multiple discovery—that

[3] Robert K. Merton, "Priorities in scientific discovery: a chapter in the sociology of science," *American Sociological Review*, 22 (1957), 635; "Singletons and multiples in scientific discovery: a chapter in the sociology of science," *Proceedings of the American Philosophical Society*, 105 (October, 1961), 470.

is, discovery by two or more individuals working separately—occurs with remarkable frequency, that it often gives rise to disputes for priority among the parties concerned, and that these disputes may be laced with the bitterest and most violent passions of which the protagonists are capable. Several important things about the life of science may be learned from this analysis.

First, the multiplicity of discovery runs so high in so many cases that one is almost persuaded that it is a widespread occurrence rather than a chance rarity. As Galton remarks, "When apples are ripe they fall readily." One may go further, as Kuhn [4] has done, and remark that although some discoveries, such as x rays or oxygen, take one completely by surprise, there are many, many more which are more or less expected, and toward which several people are working simultaneously. It is in the latter class that we experience the multiple discovery and the disputed priority, though probably the disputants would hotly contest that their prize discovery was in no wise expected and that their opponent had either stolen the idea or had discovered only inadvertently a part of the essential new matter.

The figures cited by Merton and Barber [5] for the historical incidence of multiple discovery in various degrees enable us to test, in a fashion highly instructive, the "ripe apple" model. If there are 1000 apples on a tree, and 1000 blindfolded men reach up at random to pick an apple, what is the chance of a man's getting one to himself, or finding himself grasping as well the hand of another picker, or even more than one? This is a straightforward question in statistical probability. By means of

[4] Thomas S. Kuhn, "Historical structure of scientific discovery," *Science*, 136 (June 1, 1962), 760.

[5] Cited in Merton, *Proceedings of the American Philosophical Society*, 105 (October, 1961), 483 left.

the Poisson distribution it is found that 368 men will be successful and that 264 cases will involve the remaining 632 men in contested claims (Table 3).

TABLE 3
POISSON DISTRIBUTION AND SIMULTANEOUS DISCOVERY

Number of simultaneous discoverers	Merton data cases	1000 apples and men cases
0	Indeterminate	368
1	No data	368
2	179	184
3	51	61
4	17	15
5	6	3
6 or more	8	1

The agreement between expectation and fact, at least for the doublet, triplet, and quadruplet discoveries, is striking but must not be given too much credence. To fit the data we have made two arbitrary assumptions: first, that we start with 1000 pickers or discoverers; second, that there shall be on the average one prize for each. The first assumption is reasonable, for one cannot avoid adjusting the data to some sort of total population. The second is harder to justify, especially as it involves 368 apples that were not picked at all, discoveries that were missed because of the overlapping hands. As a first approximation, however, we note that only 37 percent of the seekers will establish uncontested claims, the remaining 63 percent will end in multiple discovery. In terms of actual discoveries made, the position is a little brighter: about 58 percent will be unique, and only 42 percent will be shared by two or more.

As a second approximation, the data show more instances

than we expect by random choice involving five or more coin-
cident pickers of the same discovery. Perhaps the apples that
appear to be biggest and most ready to drop attract more than
their due share of the pickers, but this is only a minor amend-
ment to the gross phenomenon.

Not all cases of multiple discovery end in hotly contested priority disputes. Merton shows that the tendency has decreased
as we have become used to the idea that this is bound to happen, the proportion of disputes being 92 percent in the seventeenth century, 72 percent in the eighteenth, 59 percent by the
latter half of the nineteenth, and 33 percent in the first half of
the present century.

Even at these rates, the passion generated and the large
amount of overlapping discovery that seems to have been with
us throughout the recorded history of the scientific paper makes
us wary of the role of that device. If it is for front-line communication, then we must feel that it has always done a remarkably poor job of preventing overlapping researches. The apple-
pickers appear to act as if they were blindfolded to the efforts
of others rather than as if they had any information in time for
them to move their hands to one of the many untouched fruits.
If paper publication is not for front-line communication, let us
cease to complain about overlapping.

The scientific paper therefore seems to arise out of the claim-
staking brought on by so much overlapping endeavor. The social origin is the desire of each man to record his claim and
reserve it to himself. Only incidentally does the paper serve as
a carrier of information, an announcement of new knowledge
promulgated for the good of the world, a giving of free advantage to all one's competition. Indeed, in past centuries it was
not uncommon for a Galileo, Hooke, or Kepler to announce his
discovery as a cryptogram of jumbled letters that reserved

priority without conferring the information that would help his rivals. In the present day, as Reif has pointed out, the intense competition to publish "fustest and mostest" and thereby achieve prestige has resulted in a long series of abuses and high emotions ranging from illicit publication in the New York *Times* to rare cases of fraudulent claim.[6]

Why the scientist acts in this way is another question. The answer to it, I feel, may involve some rather deep psychological analysis of the scientific character. At the root of the matter is the basic difference that exists between creative effort in the sciences and in the arts.[7] If Michelangelo or Beethoven had not existed, their works would have been replaced by quite different contributions. If Copernicus or Fermi had never existed, essentially the same contributions would have had to come from other people. There is, in fact, only one world to discover, and as each morsel of perception is achieved, the discoverer must be honored or forgotten. The artist's creation is intensely personal, whereas that of the scientist needs recognition by his peers. The ivory tower of the artist can be a one-man cell; that of the scientist must contain many apartments so that he may be housed among his peers.

Two important implications emerge from this analysis. First, scientific communication by way of the published paper is and always has been a means of settling priority conflicts by claim-staking rather than avoiding them by giving information. Second, claims to scientific property are vital to the make-up of the scientist and his institutions. For these reasons scientists

[6] F. Reif, "The competitive world of the pure scientist," *Science,* 134 (December 15, 1961), 1957–62.

[7] A beginning for such analysis has been made by Karl W. Deutsch, "Scientific and Humanistic Knowledge in the Growth of Civilization," in *Science and the Creative Spirit* (Toronto, Ont., University of Toronto Press, 1958), pp. 3–51.

have a strong urge to write papers but only a relatively mild one to read them. For these reasons there is a considerable social organization of scientists whose aim is to establish and secure the prestige and priority they desire by means more efficient than the traditional device of journal publication.

When one talks about the information problem in science, it is, I feel, important not to confuse the matter with that which we have just described. For three centuries science has lived effectively with the high incidence of multiple discovery and disputed claims for priority. At every turn in past history it was to be regretted that X's ideas were not known to Y. The overlapping could hardly have been worse, and there is no clear evidence that it has ever either improved or deteriorated.

Perhaps it is not just the counsel of despair to posit that science has lived vigorously if not happily on its diet of disputes and duplications. Perhaps it is even desirable that many of the important discoveries should be made two or three times over in an independent and slightly different fashion. Perhaps men must themselves recreate such discoveries before they can usefully and effectively go on to the next stage. We seem nowadays to dispute less about the same amount of overlapping, but perhaps we have only turned our wrath against the societies, publishers, librarians, and editors who seem to conspire to leave us in such a duplication-prone position. However, let us be fair. We may complain that they have not removed this stumbling block from our path, but we cannot well complain that it has grown worse. It could hardly be worse. Our information problem, assuming we have one, is of a different nature.

Let us first look at the organization problem of scientific literature in terms of the input and output of any one man. We have seen that the normal scientist may during his lifetime publish papers ranging in number from a minimal one up to several hundred and that the borderline between many and few is about the geometric mean between these limits. Consider now how much he must read in order to produce those papers. At the beginning of his career, his teachers and his basic reading of books and current literature in a chosen subject will have placed him at the research front, and from there he will perhaps be able to voyage alone on uncharted seas. If this man remains in a field of which he is the sole exponent, he can read nothing besides his own papers. Such is the life of the lone pioneer who has no need to read journals and publishes (if he does) only for the good of future generations.

But life is usually not like that. The man arriving at the research front finds others with the same basic training in the same subject looking at the same problems and trying to pick apples off the same tree. He will want to monitor the work of these similar individuals who are his rivals and his peers. He will want to leapfrog over their advances rather than duplicate them. How many such individuals can be so handled? I suggest that the answer is on the order of a hundred. Surely he can read one paper for every one he writes. Just as surely, he cannot efficiently monitor 10,000 papers for each one of his own, at which rate the good man who writes 100 papers in a lifetime would be reading a million, or more than 60 a day.

Another way of deriving this ratio is to think of the number of people with whom a good scientist can exchange offprints and preprints, professional correspondence, and with whom he can perhaps collaborate at a reasonable and comprehensive level. Publishers have their records of the purchase of reprints, but I know of no published figures. My guess is that there are a few hundred colleagues for every worker. Here, of course, we are dealing with numbers of *actual* men rather than with numbers of papers due to *effective* men. We do read several papers by people who are not on our lists, after all, and correspondingly ignore some of the output by our friends.

There is yet another way of looking at this ratio. The norm of the number of papers given as references in a research paper has for many years been constant at a little less than ten. Supposing we read, closely enough to cite them, about 10 papers for every one we actually cite, there would then have been about 100 papers read for every one published. Our tendency to faithfully repeat citations of our favorite and most useful papers only reduces this figure.

It seems then that we can handle an effective input that is little more than a few hundred times the size of our output. Perhaps those who write little have more time for reading than those who are prolific, so that there is some sort of balance. Perhaps the true research man does not read at all but takes his input in other ways, orally and socially. On the whole, one can keep up with a colleague group that has an effective size of a few hundred members; one cannot possibly keep up with 10,000.[8]

However, since all aspects of science grow exponentially with the remarkable rapidity of a factor of 10 in 50 years, it seems clear that when a subject has reached the stage where its first dozen protagonists are beginning to feed on one another's papers and to watch their priorities and advances, it can scarcely be expected to remain intact as a field for another generation. When in the course of natural growth it

[8] One may however *scan* a group of this size or even larger—using, say, one of the abstracts journals, in order to find the small group.

begins sensibly to exceed the few hundred members postulated, each man will find himself unable to monitor the field properly.

At each stage along the way the backlog of papers can be packed down into review articles and eventually into textbooks. For example, the progenitor of such a field, looking back at the end of his working life upon, say, 100 papers of his own and an effective list equivalent to 100 colleagues, can muster a bibliography of 10,000 items, duly compressed into a critical review of the state of the art. But this never solves the current problem of more than several hundred men trying to keep up with one another's work.

One of the traditional modes of expression among such groups is the founding of a new scientific organ, a journal which is their medium for communication. A membership of several hundred may be augmented by a thousand or more individuals only fractionally or marginally within the group. Add to this the subscription list of the libraries which decide that the journal is necessary to them and the usual quota of miscellaneous subventions, and one has an economic modicum for such a publishing endeavor.

This gives us, incidentally, a check on our ratio of 100. Since science began, about 10 million scientific papers have been published, and we are adding to them, with a doubling in 10 years, or about 6 percent a year, about 600,000 new papers every year. These come out in some 30,000 current journals, which therefore each carry an average of 20 per year. Now 10 million papers implies the existence of about three million authors, most of whom, because of exponential growth, are alive now. Therefore, there is approximately one journal for every 100 authors. Since the seventeenth century, the besetting sin of all journal creators has been to imagine that theirs was a journal to end all journals in that particular realm of subject matter.[9] One doubts whether any group like the audience of such a journal has remained a closed set beyond the appearance of the first issue. Members of the group invariably read more papers than those prescribed for them by their colleague editor. Moreover, members of other groups find that their diet can be improved by reciprocal poaching. Thus, although there is an average of only 100 scientists to each journal, nevertheless, it will reach about 1000 scientists if each man looks at 10 serials.

Such overlapping, as in multiple discovery, generates heat and lowers efficiency. What is sought is the adiabatic expansion that could be had if science could be compartmented into watertight areas, that is, if a man in one area need never extend his reasearch reading into any other. But evidently science abhors such splitting. Even the splitting of chemistry from physics when the cake of natural philosophy was divided gave rise automatically to disciplines of physical chemistry and chemical physics, so that each section needed constant surveillance of the others adjacent. Overlap of research fields is a sort of embargo that nature exerts against the urge that man has to divide and conquer.

As might be expected, journals are not shared with 10 men reading each issue or each paper. A now classical paper by Urquhart [10] analyzed the crop during 1956 of 53,000 external loan requests filled by the (central) Science Library

[9] One might well look into the motivation of such founders. Compare the story in which two little girls seize control of their fourth-grade discussion club by a method that they described as "the fair and square way by which any group takes over any club—capture of the mimeograph machine."

[10] D. J. Urquhart, "Use of Scientific Periodicals," International Conference on Scientific Information, National Academy of Sciences–National Research Council, Washington, D.C., 1958, pp. 277–90, Tables II, VII.

in London from its holdings of 9120 different scientific periodicals, of which more than 1300 were not current (Fig. 17). More than 4800 of the current titles were not used at all during the year; 2274 were used only once. At the other end of the scale, the most popular journal had 382 requests, 60 titles were requested more than 100 times each, and half the requests could be met from the top 40 journals. Less than 10 percent of the available serials were sufficient to meet 80 percent of the demand.

This distribution in rank of journals is equivalent to that which we have already met in scientific productivity. There is the same Pareto curve as in the distributions of incomes or sizes of cities, apparently for much the same reasons. Thus, journal-dwellers are distributed in the same way as city-dwellers; there is the same tendency to crystallize, and the same balance between the exponential growth of the largest members and the increasing numbers of the smallest. Since the dividing line is drawn at the square root of the total population, we can say that although 30,000 journals exist, half the reading that is done uses only the 170 most popular items.

Amount of use seems intuitively to be a better test of quality than our former criterion, amount of productivity. Unfortunately, though we now have figures for the utility of journals in terms of their rate of usage by a large population, we have no comparable figures for individual papers. It seems almost inevitable on qualitative grounds alone that the same conditions would apply, and that there would be a Pareto-like distribution linking a hierarchy of most popular papers at the top end of the scale with a low-ranking group used twice, or once, or perhaps never.

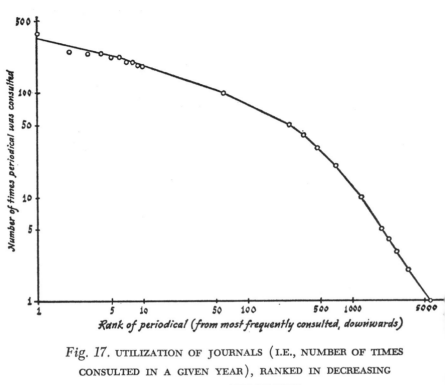

Fig. 17. UTILIZATION OF JOURNALS (I.E., NUMBER OF TIMES
CONSULTED IN A GIVEN YEAR), RANKED IN DECREASING
ORDER OF UTILIZATION

In this study, more than 3000 of the available total of 9120 journals in
the library were not called for at all during the period of investigation.

From this it would follow that all statements hitherto made about the numbers of good researchers vis-à-vis poor researchers would apply if we had data for a true count of quality rather than the admittedly crude count of quantity. We know that the ranks of individuals would not by any means correspond on the two scales, but one could say with some assurance that there would be a significant correlation between qualitative solidness and quantitative solidness. However, since it is fortunately not incumbent upon us to provide such measures for individuals, all we need is the knowledge that the statistical mechanics of scientific manpower and literature obey such general laws.[11]

It also follows from the existence of these stable and regular distribution curves that we may now justify on a theoretical basis our previously empirical procedure of using crude numbers of periodicals or papers as an index of the size of science. We know now that any measure of total number of journals, papers, or men will give the corresponding number of important journals, papers, or people. It will be seen that a slight change in definition—for example, uncertainty about the minimum allowable level at which a journal may be accounted scientific—will only increase the size of the tail. This is why even the loosest definitions yield usable results and regular exponential growths.

Having posited that amount of usage provides a reasonable measure of the scientific importance of a journal or a man's work, let us apply this to the scientific paper in general. Let

[11] At this point most scientists will express disappointment. I suspect they have a secret hope that some standard will be found for the objective judgment of their own caliber and reputation. This craving for a recognition unsullied by human subjectivity is in itself an interesting psychological phenomenon.

us consider the use of a paper in terms of the references made to it in other papers. We shall have to ignore the evident malpractice of some authors in preferentially citing their own papers, those of their special friends, or those of powerful or important scientists that confer status on their work. We shall also take a rosy view in supposing that the practice of first writing the paper and then adding for decoration some canonical quota of a dozen references—like Greek pillars on a Washington, D.C., building—does not sensibly pervert the average conscientiousness in giving credit to papers that have provided the foundation for the work.

We suppose, then, that a research contribution is built from a man's own work, from a corpus of common knowledge needing no specific citation, and from an average of 10 other papers to which reference is made. Take now a field in which since the beginning of time a total of N papers has been published. If that field is doubling every decade, as healthy fields do, the next year will produce an additional crop of $0.07 N$ papers, and these will contain $0.7 N$ references to the backlog of N papers. On an average, then, each of the N papers will be cited by new ones at the rate of 0.7 times per year. We have supposed, however, that the incidence of citation and referencing, since these measure the utility of the various papers, cannot be spread out uniformly. Some papers will be cited much more than others. Some may fall unnoticed and never be cited.[12]

Let us look first at the way in which citation appears to

[12] Papers behave rather like a human population, except that it seems to take a quorum of about 10 papers to produce a new one, rather than a pair of male and female. We have now shown that childbearing proceeds at constant rate.

fall off with age. It has been remarked several times [13] that if all the references cited in a single issue of a journal, or the volume for a certain year, are sorted according to date, then the number falls off rapidly as one goes back in time. Fussler [14] investigated physics and chemistry journals of various dates and showed that although papers as old as 150 years had been cited, there was clearly a falling-off with age. Half of all references in chemistry were made to papers less than eight years old, half in physics to papers published in the preceding five years. Unfortunately, the data are badly upset by his use of the war years 1919 and 1946 as half of the sample.

A better analysis of the useful half-life of papers can be made from the librarians' investigations of the amount of use given the various bound volumes of their runs of periodicals (Fig. 18). In the greater libraries, among large populations of such journals, it has been found several times that the use falls off by a factor of two in times on the order of nine years. The data of Gross and Gross [15] on references made in a single volume (1926) of *Chemical Literature*, show a halving of the number for every 15 years of increased age.

Although this falling away is striking, remember that the actual amount of literature in each field is growing expo-

[13] See, for example, J. H. Westbrook, "Identifying significant research," *Science*, 132 (October 28, 1960), 1229–34. Also Paul Weiss, "Knowledge, a growth process," *Science*, 131 (June 3, 1960), 1716, and the clarifying subsequent discussion by S. J. Goffard and C. D. Windle, *Science*, 132 (September 2, 1960), 625.

[14] Herman H. Fussler, "Characteristics of the research literature used by chemists and physicists in the United States," *Library Quarterly*, 19 (1949), 19–35; 20 (1950), 119–143.

[15] P. L. K. Gross and E. M. Gross, "College libraries and chemical education," *Science*, 66 (October 28, 1927), 385–89.

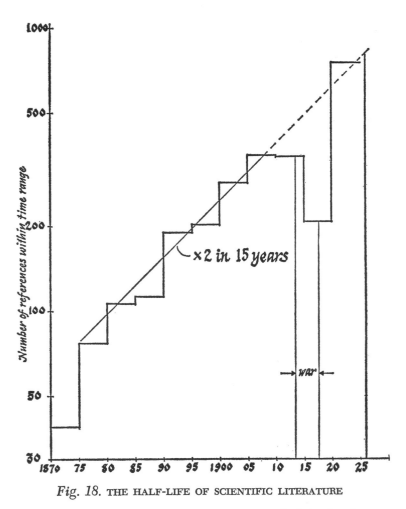

Fig. 18. THE HALF-LIFE OF SCIENTIFIC LITERATURE

Count from a 1926 volume of a scientific periodical of the distribution by date of all references cited in that volume. It will be noted that with the exception of a five-year period embracing World War I, the number of references falls off by a factor of two in 15 years.

nentially and therefore doubling every 10 to 15 years. Therefore, to a first approximation, the number of references of a given date seem to rest in proportion to the total literature available at that date. Thus, although half the literature cited will in general be less than a decade old, it is clear that, roughly speaking, any paper once it is published will have a constant chance of being used at all subsequent dates.[16]

This rather surprising result may be modified in improving our approximation. In fields tending to honor their pioneers by eponymic fame—name laws, name constants, name species —one may find that good papers actually improve with age, and their chance of citation increases. In fields embarrassed by an inundation of literature there will be a tendency to bury as much of the past as possible and to cite older papers less often than is their statistical due. This tendency can be seen in the journal *Physical Review Letters*, which achieves the greatest possible rapidity of publication.

In these *Letters*, since their foundation, the half-life of references has been stable at about 2½ years; that is to say, half of all references are younger than that. Now, the past 2½ years of physics literature contains less than one-third of all the work published during the last decade, and that decade, of course, contains half of all that has ever been printed. The people publishing in these letters are thus enabled by rapid publication to deal with less than one-third of all the papers that would normally be involved. To balance this, papers in the field must necessarily be cited something like three times as frequently, and therefore the amount of overlapping of citations is much increased.

[16] In fact a constant rate of citation will ensure that the field increases with compound interest so that the growth is exponential.

Now, papers which make the same citations have an increased likelihood of doing the same work. Thus, increasing the efficiency of the rate at which one can make priority claims automatically seems to produce a higher incidence of such claims, or at least of the raw material for them. There is a feedback working to minimize part of the advantage gained by rapid publication.[17]

Let us look next at the way that references and citations are distributed other than in terms of date. If we were to rank any population of papers in terms of a hierarchy having at the top the most-cited paper of the year and at the bottom those given as a reference only once or not at all, we should evidently have a Pareto-type distribution similar to that found for the utility of scientific journals. In terms of this we might, if we had the information, say that half of all citations were given to a small group of papers existing at that time. On purely qualitative grounds one would suppose that 100 papers out of a field of 10,000 supply about one-third of the citations. On the other hand there will inevitably be several thousand papers that are lost, or cited so rarely that they do not become generally known. It is impossible to say how much of this loss is deserved and just, but a large body of jilted authors will feel that it is not. There are cautionary tales of rediscovered papers, like that of Mendel, to make us feel that the statistical loss of literature must be minimized.

Thus, the essential problems of scientific manpower and

[17] I therefore arrive at the conclusion that a scientific race to get there first is tremendously wasteful, and that anything that lessens the reward for such achievement is good. Thus it is perhaps a good thing to deprive the authors of their chance to get their names on the paper. It might be made sufficient honor and reward that they are allowed to play with the team.

literature are twofold. At the top the critical problem is predominantly one of human engineering: arranging for the highest level people to interact in manageable numbers, seeing that the great journals continue to correspond to large natural groups, arranging for the important papers to be collected and compressed into standard monographs and texts. At the lower end it is one of switchboard operation: how does one manage the large body of average scientists and appliers so that it keeps pace with the leaders; how does one monitor the lesser journals and the almost unnoticed papers so as to prevent wastage? We shall see several different mechanisms at work, each of them presently in a critical condition, as we make the logistic transition from Little Science to Big Science.

The first noteworthy phenomenon of human engineering is that new groups of scientists emerge, groups composed of our maximal 100 colleagues. In the beginning, when no more than this number existed in a country, they could compose themselves as the Royal Society or the American Philosophical Society. At a later stage, they could split into specialist societies of this size. Now, even the smallest branches of subject matter tend to exceed such membership, and the major groups contain tens and hundreds of thousands. In a group of such size, by our previous analysis, there are likely to be a few groups of magnitude 100, each containing a set of interacting leaders. We see now such groups emerging, somewhat bashfully, as separate entities.

Probably during World War II, pressure of circumstances forced us to form such knots of men and keep them locked away in interacting seclusion. We gave them a foretaste of urgent collaboration in nuclear physics, and again in radar. These groups are still with us in the few hundred people who meet in the "Rochester Conference" for fundamental particles studies, and in the similar number who congregate by invitation to discuss various aspects of solid state physics.

The organization is not perfect; a few of the best men may not attend, a few of those who do attend might not qualify if we had perfect objective judgment. Conscientiously, one might try not to be too exclusive, not to bar the gentleman from Baffinland who would be a distinguished researcher on fundamental particles if only he could. But there is a limit to the useful size, and, if too many are invited, an unofficial subgroup of really knowledgeable members will be forced into being.

Such activity is by no means confined to the two groups mentioned. Similar unofficial organizations exist in molecular biology, in computer theory, in radio astronomy, and doubtless in all sciences with tens of thousands of participants. By our theory they are inevitable, and not just a product of the war or the special character of each discipline. Conferences are just one symptom; it becomes insufficient to meet as a body every year, and there is a need for a more continuous means of close contact with the group of a hundred.

And so these groups devise mechanisms for day-to-day communication. There is an elaborate apparatus for sending out not merely reprints of publications but preprints and prepreprints of work in progress and results about to be achieved.[18] The existence of such a group might be diagnosed by checking the preprint list of one man and following this by a check of the list of each man mentioned. I think one would soon

---

[18] Like government contract research reports, these represent an obnoxious (though historically interesting) back-door means of getting publication for a mass of writing that might be better lost.

find a closed group, a small number of hundreds in member-ship strength, selected from a population of a large number of tens of thousands.

In addition to the mailing of preprints, ways and means are being found for physical juxtaposition of the members. They seem to have mastered the art of attracting invitations from centers where they can work along with several members of the group for a short time. This done, they move on to the next center and other members. Then they return to home base, but always their allegiance is to the group rather than to the institution which supports them, unless it happens to be a station on such a circuit. For each group there exists a sort of commuting circuit of institutions, research centers, and summer schools giving them an opportunity to meet piece-meal, so that over an interval of a few years everybody who is anybody has worked with everybody else in the same category.

Such groups constitute an invisible college, in the same sense as did those first unofficial pioneers who later banded together to found the Royal Society in 1660. In exactly the same way, they give each man status in the form of approba-tion from his peers, they confer prestige, and, above all, they effectively solve a communication crisis by reducing a large group to a small select one of the maximum size that can be handled by interpersonal relationships. Such groups are to be encouraged, for they give status pay-off without increasing the papers that would otherwise be written to this end. I think one must admit that high-grade scientific commuting has become an important channel of communication, and that we must ease its progress.

Possibly, if such groups were made legitimate, recognized, and given newspaperlike broadsheet journals circulating to a few hundred individuals, this would spoil them, make them objects of envy or of high-handed administration and formality. Elite scientific newspapers or broadsheets of this sort have long existed in Japan, a country faced with the special problem that many of its top scientists spend appreciable periods in foreign institutes.

The scientific elite have acquired prestige among the public in general and the employers in particular, which has given them a certain affluence and enabled them to commute. It incidentally replaces the kudos they have lost since the debasement of the coinage of scientific publication. Despite a tendency to place summer schools in pleasant resort areas whenever possible and to make institute housing a good place to bring one's family, there is a further need. There is a further need to recognize that although a place such as Brookhaven was once where one went to work with big machines and certain other facilities, it has come nowadays to play an increasingly important role as a station on the commuting circuit of several invisible colleges. People come to work with other people, who have come to work with yet other people, who happen to be there. We need many more such facilities in various fields and in various countries. It might, for example, be wise for the United States government to subsidize the erection of "Fulbright residential buildings" in London, Cambridge and Oxford, Copenhagen, Geneva, Paris, Delhi, and wherever else United States scientists habitually commute in quantity.

So much for the elite, what of the masses? Mention of the big machines is immediately reminiscent of one way in which the formation of elites is producing a problem in the organization of the rest of the scientific population. It has become common to organize research, especially big machine work, around quite a large team of men comprising a few leaders in various specialties and a large number of younger men. Now it becomes the custom to publish as just such a team. As an editor of *Physical Review Letters* plaintively noted on a recent occasion, "The participating physicists are not mentioned, not even in a footnote." [19]

Surprisingly enough, a detailed examination of the incidence of collaborative work in science shows that this is a phenomenon which has been increasing steadily and ever more rapidly since the beginning of the century (Fig. 19). It is hard to find any recent acceleration of the curves that would correspond to the coming of the big machine and indicate this as a recognizable contributing cause.

Data from *Chemical Abstracts* [20] show that in 1900 more than 80 percent of all papers had a single author, and almost all the rest were pairs, the greater number being those signed by a professor and his graduate student, though a few are of the type Pierre and Marie Curie, Cockcroft and Walton, Sherlock Holmes and Dr. Watson.[21] Since that time the proportion of multi-author papers has accelerated steadily and

[19] S. A. Goudsmit, *Physical Review Letters*, 8 (March 15, 1962), 229. Another good example of a quite different sort of collaboration is the appearance of the world's greatest pseudonymous mathematician, Nicolas Bourbaki. This Frenchman with a Greek name, author of an internationally famous collection of treatises on modern higher mathematics, is actually a group of 10 to 20 mathematicians, most of them French, all of them highly eminent in their fields, none of them identified by name as part of the polycephalic Bourbaki. See Paul R. Halmos, "Nicolas Bourbaki," *Scientific American*, 196 (May, 1957), 88–99.

[20] Results of an unpublished investigation by L. Badash, Yale University.

[21] L. Kowarski, "Team work and individual work in research," *CERN Courier*, 2 (May, 1962), 4–7.

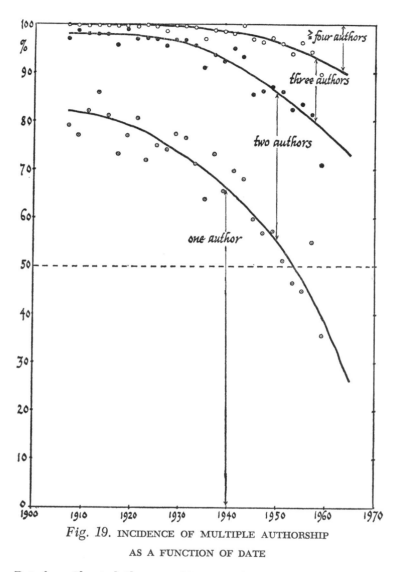

Fig. 19. INCIDENCE OF MULTIPLE AUTHORSHIP

AS A FUNCTION OF DATE

Data from *Chemical Abstracts*, 1910–60, are here presented showing the percentages of papers having a single author, those with two, three, and four or more. It seems evident that there has been a steadily accelerating change since the beginning of the century.

powerfully, and it is now so large that if it continues at the present rate, by 1980 the single-author paper will be extinct.[22] It is even more impressive that three-author papers are accelerating more rapidly than two-author, four-author more rapidly than three-author papers, and so on. At present only about one paper in four has a multiplicity of three or more authors, but, if the trend holds, more than half of all papers will be in this category by 1980 and we shall move steadily toward an infinity of authors per paper. It is one of the most violent transitions that can be measured in recent trends of scientific manpower and literature.

One way of understanding this movement toward mass collaboration is to see it as a natural extension of the growth created by the constant shift of the Pareto distribution of scientific productivities. There is a continuous movement toward an increase in the productivity of the most prolific authors and an increase in the numbers of those minimally prolific. As we approach a limit in both directions, it is clear that something has to give. The most prolific people increase their productivities by being the group leaders of teams that can accomplish more than they could singly. The minimal group are in short supply and we can hardly afford

[22] Cf. data for *Mathematical Reviews* and three United States mathematics journals (percent papers having joint authors):

	Math. Revs.	Three U.S. journals
1920		2.2
1930		4.1
1940	5.8	18.2
1950	6.5	18.2
1960	10.8	12.7

From a letter by W. R. Utz, *American Mathematical Society Notices*, 9 (1962), 196–97.

to let them grow until they reach that ripeness of producing significant papers on their own. By the creation of a class of fractional authors—that is, scientists who produce one nth part of a scientific paper—a much larger number of the minimal group is kept at the lower end of the distribution. One expects that as these individuals grow they will evolve into unit authors or better, but in the meantime the body of research workers is increased to meet demand. It is to some extent accidental that wartime organization and the advent of the big machine have occasioned the introduction of fractionality, without which we should have a severe manpower shortage.

A more optimistic viewpoint to take is that the emergence of this class of sorcerer's apprentices partly solves the problem of organizing the lower-level scientists so that they can be directly related to the research life of the elite. This is nothing but a logical extension of that old familiar principle, the great professor with his entourage of graduate students, the sort of thing for which Rutherford or Liebig are well known. The great difference here is that the apex of the triangle is not a single beloved individual but an invisible college; its locale is not a dusty attic of a teaching laboratory but a mobile commuting circle of rather expensive institutions. R. E. Weston *et al.* have suggested that one might name such teams as the Dubna Reds and the Harvard M.I.T. Yankees, and give each player a rating.[23]

Because of this, one of the great consequences of the transition from Little Science to Big Science has been that after three centuries the role of the scientific paper has drastically changed. In many ways the modern ease of transportation and the affluence of the elite scientist have replaced what used to

[23] Letter in *Physics Today*, 15 (June, 1962), 79–80.

be effected by the publication of papers. We tend now to communicate person to person instead of paper to paper. In the most active areas we diffuse knowledge through collaboration. Through select groups we seek prestige and the recognition of ourselves by our peers as approved and worthy collaborating colleagues. We publish for the small group, forcing the pace as fast as it will go in a process that will force it harder yet. Only secondarily, with the inertia born of tradition, do we publish for the world at large.

All this makes for considerable change in the motivation of the scientist; it alters his emotional attitude toward his work and his fellow scientists. It has made the scientific paper, in many ways, an art that is dead or dying. More than this, the invisible colleges have a built-in automatic feedback mechanism that works to increase their strength and power within science and in relation to social and political forces. Worse, the feedback is such that we stand in danger of losing strength and efficiency in fields and countries where the commuting circuit has not yet developed. In short, now that we have achieved a reasonably complete theory of scientific manpower and literature, we must look to the social and political future.

(4)

POLITICAL STRATEGY
FOR
BIG SCIENTISTS

IN OUR ANALYSIS of the growth of science we have reached a basic understanding of normal exponential increase and distribution of talent and productivity. Now let us turn our attention to the abnormal—that is, to those things that do not follow the pattern. Without doubt, the most abnormal thing in this age of Big Science is money. The finances of science seem highly irregular and, since they dominate most of the social and political implications, our analysis must start here.

If the costliness of science were distributed in the same way as its productivity or excellence, there would be no problem. If the *per capita* cost of supporting scientists were constant, we should only spend in proportion to their number, so that the money they cost would double every 10 to 15 years. But in fact our expenditure, measured in constant dollars, doubles every 5½ years, so that the cost *per scientist* seems to have been doubling every 10 years. To put it another way, the cost of science has been increasing as the square of the number of scientists.

Since we know that in general the number of average scientists increases as the square of the number of eminent highly productive ones, we derive the frightening costly principle that research expenditure increases as the fourth power of the number of good scientists. It has already been estimated that the United States may possess enough talent to multiply the population of distinguished scientists by a factor of five. Let us be conservative and envisage a future in which it is only tripled; we could reach this point quite some time before the year 2000. By then, according to the principle just derived, our expenditure would have multiplied by a factor of 81, and would thus be more than double our entire Gross National Product.

It seems incontrovertible that such an increase in the cost of science has been taking place. National research and development expenditures were about three billion dollars in 1950 and thirteen billion dollars in 1960—more than a doubling every five years. The 15 percent annual increase must be matched against a rise in the Gross National Product of only $3\frac{1}{2}$ percent a year. At the present rate, science will be 10 percent of the Gross National Product as early as 1973. It is already in the region 2 to 3 percent, depending on definition.

Let us be optimistic and suppose that growth of the Gross National Product will continue, with no manpower shortage to impede the increase in the number of qualified scientists, and return to the question of whether the cost per scientist must also increase. Data from the federal agencies that now support so much research indicate clearly that the cost per project has been rising rapidly. The National Institutes of Health figures for average expenditure per project are $9,649 in 1950 and $18,584 in 1960, almost a doubling.[1] Johnson and

[1] Dale R. Lindsay and Ernest M. Allen, "Medical research: past support, future directions," *Science*, 134 (December 22, 1961), 2017–24.

Milton investigated the records of a wide range of research carried on in industry, universities, and government institutions [2] and found that in a decade, although the total costs increased by a factor of $4\frac{1}{2}$, the output of research and development no more than doubled.

Basically it appears that as more and more research is done our habitual and expected increase therein is still needed but becomes more difficult to obtain. The result is that we offer more and more inducement by raising salaries, providing more assistance, and giving the researchers better tools for the job. This is essentially the Fechner law situation already described, the effect being proportional to the logarithm of the stimulus. However, apparently it is necessary to use up units of financial solidness about twice as fast as units of scientific solidness.

We may now inquire why the cost of research on a *per capita* basis and in terms of the Gross National Product seems to have remained constant throughout history until about World War II and only since that time has met with the new circumstance of an increase that keeps pace with the growth of scientific manpower.

Let me offer as an interpretation, not an answer, the suggestion that this is the cybernetic feedback that is now trying to decelerate science and bring it to a maximum size. This, we maintain, is the prime cause of the present logistic rather than exponential curve. This is the difference between Big Science and Little Science. But we cannot discover the reason until we have looked deeper into the world rather than the national situation, and into the motivation of the scientist.

Let us first examine the world situation, considering all the separate countries and the various bodies of science contained

[2] Reported editorially in *Science*, 132 (August 26, 1960), 517.

in them. For a first approximation these are normally distributed like the sizes of cities within a country, ranking from the few big ones down to the many small ones. There is uniform exponential growth, just as in cities. Just like the rank list of sizes of cities, as we watch it evolve through history, the order changes slightly, though the distribution remains stable. Over the years there is a change in which some countries alternately lead and lag behind others. It is a slow process, though the realization, as in the instance of Sputnik, can be a shock to the uninformed.

During the present century, world science has altered its national divisions almost systematically. Consider the figures showing the contributions of various countries to the production of scientific papers analyzed in *Chemical Abstracts* (Fig. 20). At one end, the old and stable scientific culture of the British Commonwealth has been sensibly constant, and that of France has suffered a slight but steady decline. At the other end, the U.S.S.R., Japan, and, indeed, all the minor scientific countries, have spectacularly improved their world position from about 10 percent at the beginning of the century to nearly 50 percent now. In the middle, being squeezed by this expansion, are the two great chemical nations, Germany and the United States. Their combined share has declined from 60 to 35 percent, with the United States apparently absorbing a large part of the German share during both World Wars, and Germany having shrunk to one-fifth of its original size.

Altogether, apart from the wartime winnings from Germany, the United States has approximately maintained its relative position. It has perhaps even made up the losses of France. Remember that this does not include the steady exponential increase at the world rate of a doubling every 10

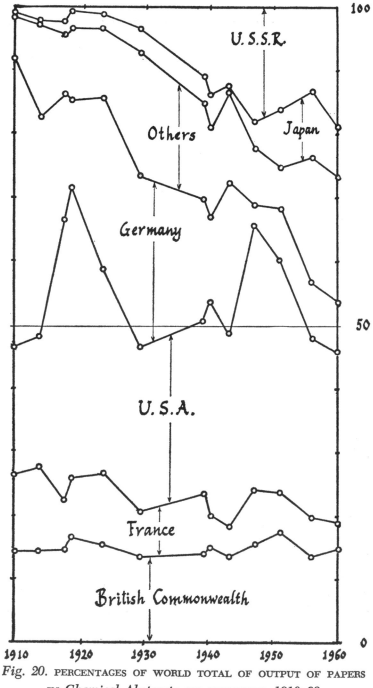

Fig. 20. PERCENTAGES OF WORLD TOTAL OF OUTPUT OF PAPERS IN *Chemical Abstracts*, BY COUNTRIES, 1910–60

years. The spectacular thing is not that the United States or any other country can maintain this rate and keep its position constant but that undeniably the U.S.S.R., Japan, and the minor scientific countries have during the present century been able to exceed this world rate so that they have grown from nonentity to a near majority. Together they seem to have erupted into the scientific scene at a rate exceeding their normal quota of the scientific explosion by about 6 percent a year. Consequently, we now face a spectacular decline in the traditional ability of big nations to form an absolute majority of science on their own. They are facing a Pareto-like distribution of smaller countries whose total bulk will soon outnumber that of the United States and U.S.S.R.

Japan, the U.S.S.R., and the United States all have present expenditures in the region of 2 to 3 percent of their Gross National Products. How is it possible that their relative productions can be shifting slowly but steadily? The likeliest explanation seems to be the steady increase in the cost of science, as society becomes saturated with this activity. A complementary effect is that it seems cheaper and easier than usual to make science explode into the "vacuum" of an underdeveloped country.

The present great activity in bringing science and its technologies to the little nation makes it worth-while for us to look more closely at the conception and birth of a modern scientific and technological civilization. We must carefully distinguish the type of scientific explosion with which we are concerned, the emergence of a country relative to all others, from the normal explosive change in which all countries are involved in proportion to their rank.

Most countries merely retain the same place in the hierarchy, complaining bitterly, like Alice, of being forced to run so hard to stay in the same place. The recent pronouncements in England of the Zuckerman Committee on scientific manpower seem to be like this. When a country decides that it can afford to let science grow only at the rate of the national economic expansion, and that the supply and demand of scientific manpower be allowed to tend to equality, this is tantamount to a suicidal withdrawal from the scientific race. Alas, it is the race that Britain, bereft of great resources of minerals or agriculture, should strive in above all else.

Since we seem to have a crystallization of science that tends to make the rich richer and the poor poorer, how does it happen that paupers occasionally turn into scientific millionaires? In one particular instance, history has provided the complete sequence of steps by which a nation suddenly emergent was able to explode more vigorously than the rest of the scientific world. An analysis of the data for Japan may stand as a prototype (Fig. 21).[3] In 1869, at the beginning of the Meiji era, ca. 1868, Japan broke with tradition and invited the introduction of Dutch science, as our Western product was then called.

Let us now trace the progress of but one science, physics. The first step was the importation of foreign science teachers from the United States and Great Britain, and the export of young Japanese students to foreign universities for advanced training. The shock wave of Western science hit the country abruptly and caused Japan's population of physicists to rise from 1 to 15 in only six years. By 1880, the shock wave had begun to die away, at first rapidly as the foreigners went home,

[3] I am grateful to Eri Yagi Shizume, Yale University, for allowing me to make use of her data, to be published in *Proceedings XII International Congress for the History of Science, Ithaca and Philadelphia, August 1962.*

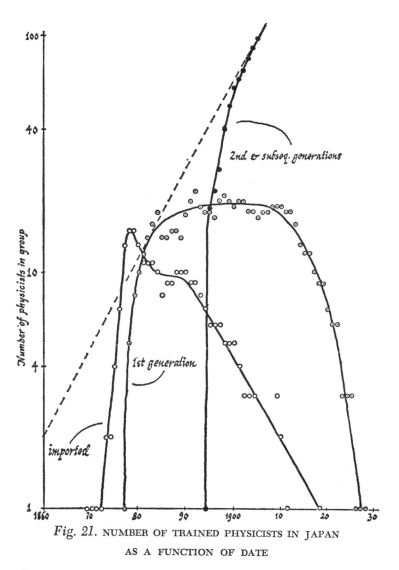

Fig. 21. NUMBER OF TRAINED PHYSICISTS IN JAPAN

AS A FUNCTION OF DATE

The "imported" curve counts Europeans and those trained in Europe. The next curve gives the numbers of their students. The third curve gives the number of Japanese students trained at home by Japanese teachers—this number grows as if it started from the original shock wave and grew exponentially to the present day, but only after a waiting period of about 15 years while the first generation was prepared.

then more slowly as foreign-trained students and teachers retired and died, so that this wave finished by 1918. But in 1880, when the imported curve was at its maximum, a new wave was rising rapidly; this was the first generation of Japanese students trained by the aforementioned foreigners and their disciples.

The first generation of students was a small group; there were 10 in 1880, and their numbers never rose above 22, reaching a stable balance between training and mortality. Later, around World War I, they begin to decline noticeably in number, the last dying in 1928.

The second generation of students, those who were now being trained by Japanese in Japan, began in 1894 and rose to 60 graduates by 1900. Shortly thereafter growth settled down to the familiar exponential pattern, doubling every 10 years. This growth, continued without serious break or disturbance, led to the state of physics in Japan through the last war.

The total effect of the shock wave and the pulse of first-generation students is the inception of exponential growth. The eventual curve of growth, projected back, acts almost exactly as if it had sprung from the crest of that first shock wave; that is, as if it had started from 12 physicists in 1881. Note, though, that growth did not start immediately; there was a lag of nearly 20 years while the second generation prepared. It seems important that the steady state arose only with this crop of entirely home-grown physicists. The picture, however, is not complete. We have omitted the important fact that primary and secondary education had also to meet similar crises at similar dates. We have neglected the crucial point that the greatest difficulty of all was to decide the language of instruction. Not until the second generation could it possibly be in their native tongue, and then not before new vocabularies and new dictionaries had been compiled.

Simplifications notwithstanding, we now have the basic time scale and the shapes of the differential equations of scientific manpower in an underdeveloped country, and we have little reason to doubt that the case is typical. Most important is the lag while waiting for a generation, then the spurt that is faster than subsequent exponential growth. It is another instance of ripe apples falling easily from the tree. The apples here are not discoveries but potentially bright physicists in a country that has no physics. This aspect is the opposite extreme from a highly developed scientific country.

The explosion of science into an underdeveloped country can, then, if serious effort is made, be much faster than into one in which science is already established. In the case of the larger population masses of the world, the process is partly familiar, and partly a cause for grave concern.

The explosion into a vacuum is basically the reason why the United States, starting its scientific revolution much later than Europe, was able to proceed more rapidly to parity and then to outpacing. In exactly the same way, the U.S.S.R., starting much later than the United States, has been able to expand at a greater exponential rate—perhaps a doubling in 7 years rather than 10. Similarly, now that China is emerging scientifically, as one can tell by the fact that we now routinely translate their chief journals as we have translated those in Russian for many years, one may expect it to reach parity perhaps within the next decade or two. The Chinese scientific population is doubling about every three years.[4]

Thus, for the great blocks of the world population we have

[4] U.S.S.R.	1950	approx.	500 journals
	1960		1500
China	1949		0
	1959		400

a sort of automatic handicap race. The later a country starts its determined effort to make modern science, the faster it can grow. One may therefore suppose that at some time during the next few decades we shall see a rather close finish to a race that has been running for several centuries. The older scientific countries will necessarily come to their mature state of saturation, and the newly scientific population masses of China, India, Africa, and others will arrive almost simultaneously at the finishing line.

I maintain that this process is historically inevitable and that we must therefore preserve a sense of balance, and not panic during the forthcoming waves of Sputnik-like scientific advances by countries previously regarded as second-rate in high science and technology.

Let us now consider the distribution curve for the incidence of scientific talent in a country. Although we have no objective measure for the talent latent in an underdeveloped country, it is reasonable to assume it would be spaced out in the same way as in developed countries, with relatively few high talents and a number of lesser talents increasing more and more as the minimum qualification is approached. As we have seen, the general effect of increasing the total scientific population is to multiply the lesser talents faster than the highest ones which dominate the scene and produce half of all the scientific advance.

As long as the country is relatively undeveloped, the number of scientists will be too small to need much crystallization into groups and elites, for the entire body will consist of the cream that has risen to the top. As the country develops, crystallization into groups, into scientific cities, begins, as well as the diminishing relative return of first-class scientists. Effectively, more and more of the extreme tip of the tail of the distribution curve is used up, so there is a tendency to use up a longer and longer segment of the tail, to make scientists of those nearer and nearer to the average ability.

It must be emphasized that we are not saying that there is any lowering of the minimum standards for being a scientist. Merely, it seems that the effort to gain more scientists increases the number at the lower levels at a greater rate than it does those on the higher levels. Thus, although the number of highest caliber men can always be increased, this is done at the cost of the average standard. From the nature of this process it follows that at some stage between underdevelopment and high development one ceases to skim off the cream; society begins to have to work against the natural distribution of talents. Apparently it is inevitable that increased inducements and opportunities result in a smaller and less rich crop, albeit in enough of an increase in top people to make the process definitely worth-while for a long time.

It is our thesis that the logistic decline from centuries of exponential growth takes place because we are scraping the bottom of the barrel in this way. At a certain point it may no longer be worth-while to sacrifice so much to increase inducements and opportunities when the only result is a declining over-all standard. It is a difficult thesis to maintain, for it might well be said that so long as first-class people can be produced, and so long as those already in being can be enabled to continue first-class work, it is always worth-while to spend the effort and money. This, I think, ignores the general mechanics of any approach to logistic stagnation. The forces of growth, deprived of their customary booty, begin to apply themselves elsewhere, and a host of new troubles result. In scientific manpower, if we begin to scrape the bottom of the barrel, this shows up in several different ways. Perhaps the most apparent is an upsetting of the traditional and natural balance among fields and among countries. The tradition depended on the natural hierarchy of growths in the various areas; the new position, instead, largely depends on the hierarchy of forces associated with logistic decelerations.

In fields of scientific activity where once there was a natural sorting of people into various subjects according to their predilections and the caprice of opportunity and inspiration, society now offers various inducements and facilities designed to attract men to specific areas. Thus, the law of supply and demand begins to obey these different forces and the distribution changes just as effectively as if there were only a constant supply and a rapidly increasing demand. There is, indeed, the equivalent of a restricted supply of the highest talent manpower, so that there is increased competition to secure a high concentration of such talent in the midst of the decreasing density of it.

Thus, in this competitive situation, fields of high inducement gain on the low in a manner deviating from the tradition. In the United States and in England at present, it is easy to see such competition between glamor subjects that get the men, and unglamorous ones that do not. There is an apparent falling away from the expected growth rates of graduate training in medicine, engineering, and education, which may be attributed to their maintenance in physics, mathematics, and astronomy.

Similarly, on the international scene, there appears to be a tendency for scientists to leave the countries where only minimal inducements and opportunities are needed to produce manpower and move to lands where in order to get the job done it must be made enormously attractive, notably the United States. The very internationality of science perhaps makes such movement more possible for scientists than it is for other classes of men. Thus, the countries of the British Commonwealth and Europe complain bitterly of their loss of high-talent manpower through emigration; and we suffer the troubles consequent upon a flow from regions of scarcity to regions of plenty, and upon crystallization of the world's supply of the mother liquor of scientific manpower which causes such manpower to aggregate in already overflowing centers.[5]

Exactly the same process takes place among disciplines as among countries. Let us analyze it further in terms of the structure we have already found, the formation of small invisible colleges of a hundred or so men outstanding in each major field. As such a group develops into an integrated body, increasing its efficiency and ability to coordinate the activities of a large number of men and their projects, so the power of the group seems to increase even more rapidly than its size. Certainly, as we have seen, its expenses will grow as the square of the size. Thus, we have a phenomenon of positive feedback; the more powerful such a group becomes, the more power it can acquire. Unto him that hath seems to be given, and this automatically entails the deprivation of him that hath not.

At heart, the motivation that causes Turkish, Yugoslav, Canadian, and Brazilian scientists to emigrate to the United

[5] For a masterly and heartfelt analysis of this problem see Stevan Dedijer, "Why did Daedalus leave?" *Science*, 133 (June 30, 1961), 2047–52.

States is the same as that which induces potential students of medicine to try for a Ph.D. in physics. Big Science countries and Big Science subjects must offer additional inducement in order to maintain normal growth, and in so doing they tend to react upon Little Science and little countries.

This is as far as the present mathematical analysis of the state of science can take us, but it hardly begins to pose the most significant problems of the age of Big Science. We must next inquire within the disciplines of sociology and psychology for the explanation of the peculiar force of inducement and opportunity within the big processes of science. Having already noted that the motivation of the scientists and the role of scientific publication appear to be changed by the emergence of invisible colleges, we must examine this more closely.

If there are to be more scientists than just those who fall from the tree like ripe apples, willing to pursue their dedicated aim in any circumstances, inducements are necessary. During the past few decades in the United States and U.S.S.R., and less so in the rest of the world, there has been a marked increase in the social status of the scientist.[6] Since he was needed, since there arose some competition, there was an automatic raising of general salaries and of the research funds and facilities commanded by the prestige and the cargo cult [7] of mod-

[6] The increase of status is analyzed in Bentley Glass, "The academic scientist 1940–1960," *Science*, 132 (September 2, 1960), 598–603.

[7] The term is used by anthropologists to describe the reactions of primitive peoples to boatloads of civilization. In the Pacific Isles, in the last war, when the Navy arrived the native huts were decked with bamboo facsimiles of radar antennae, put there so that the new gods would smile on them and bring riches. [Story told by A. Hunter Dupree, "Public education for science and technology," *Science*, 134 (September 15, 1961) 717.]

ern science. We do not at present argue about whether or not the returns justify the economic, social, or political outlay. Suffice it to note that each increase in prestige produces an undoubted pay-off in increased results, but also a heightened competition that raises the stakes for the next round.

Once we are committed to paying scientists according to their value or the demand for their services, instead of giving them, as we give other dedicated groups, merely an opportunity to survive, there seems no way back. It seems to me evident that the scientists who receive the just and proper award of such recognition are not the same sort of scientists as those who lived under the old regime, in which society almost dared them to exist.

The matter would not be so worrisome if the only way to be a scientist was to be endowed with the appropriate talents; that is to say, if people became radio astronomers not by capricious circumstances or by drifting into the field, but because that is what they could do best. From modern studies of creative ability in the scientific fields it appears that general and specific types of intelligence have surprisingly little to do with the incidence of high achievement. At best, a certain rather high minimum is needed, but once over that hump the chance of becoming a scientist of high achievement seems almost random. One noted quality is a certain gift that we shall term *mavericity,* the property of making unusual associations in ideas, of doing the unexpected. The scientist tends to be the man who, in doing the word-association test, responds to "black" not with "white" but with "caviar." Such a schizoid characteristic is plain throughout the peculiarly esoteric scientific humor of Lewis Carroll, and in a thousand broadsheets and notices of laboratory bulletin boards.

We note, incidentally, that the reaction to this mavericity is what produces the also characteristic objectivity and conservatism of the good scientist, the resistance he exhibits toward discovery and mad associations found by himself and by others, the feeling that the other man must be wrong.[8] He is caught in a violent interaction of passionately free creation on the one hand and innate objective caution on the other. According to MacKinnon,[9] the highly creative scientist might almost be defined as the rare individual who can survive the acute tension between the theoretical and the esthetic, the tightrope walker between truth and beauty. Perhaps it requires an oddly stable schizophrenic trait, one made stable by becoming a scientist.

Big Science tends to restrain some expressions of mavericity. The emergence of collaborative work and invisible colleges, the very provision of excellent facilities, all work toward specific goals in research. They seem to exercise pressure to keep scientific advance directed toward those ends for which the group or project has been created. This is an old argument against the planning of research, and it always generates the response that we must be careful to give each man his head, to allow him to follow the trail wherever it might lead. But there is no way to ensure that the man will be motivated to follow the trail when prestige and status depend on recognition by the group.

When the prestige and status of an individual are sufficient,

[8] Bernard Barber, "Resistance by scientists to scientific discovery," *Science,* 134 (September 1, 1961), 596–602.

[9] Donald W. MacKinnon, "What makes a person creative?" *Saturday Review,* XLV (February 10, 1962), 15–17, 69; "The Nature and Nurture of Creative Talent," Bingham Lecture, Yale University, April 11, 1962.

or when for some other reason the whole group can be induced to follow, it makes a breakthrough, a now familiar type of phenomenon that carries high additional status with it. Although there is therefore some group encouragement of the display of mavericity, it might well be that this applies only in special cases, and that we may now be wasting mavericity in other directions. Perhaps there is need for an active effort to provide a sufficiency of support for research without objective, funding without project, means for study and status without obligation to subscribe to a specified goal, the sort of thing that is at present partially provided in institutes for advanced study and through high-status research professorships.

Returning now to the question of whether reward by Big Science produces a breed of scientist different from that of Little Science, let us look at the characteristics noted by all those who have sought regularities among groups of eminent scientists. Galton, one of the first investigators, noted that more than half of his group of distinguished scientists were the eldest or the only child in their families, and this proportion, much higher than average, has since been confirmed in several investigations. Galton noted also that an unusually high proportion of his subjects were very attached to one parent, most often the mother. In extension of this it has since been remarked that many of the great men of science lost one parent early in youth (before the age of ten) and became strongly attached to the other.[10] Case histories show that scientists often are lonely children who find it easier to relate to things than to people. In short, many peculiar charac-

[10] Newton, Kelvin, Lavoisier, Boyle, Huygens, Count Rumford, Mme. Curie, and Maxwell are examples.

teristics of personality seem to apply to those who become scientists.[11]

I suggest that all these characteristics apply to people who became eminent in the days of Little Science, and that we do not yet have much inkling of whatever new characteristics have been elicited by the changes to the new conditions of Big Science. Many of the personality traits found formerly seem to be consistent with the hypothesis that many scientists turned to their profession for an emotional gratification that was otherwise lacking. If this is true, be it only a partial explanation, one can still see how cataclysmic must be the effect of changing the emotional rewards of the scientific life. If scientists were, on the whole, relatively normal people, just perhaps more intelligent or even more intelligent in some special directions, it would not be so difficult. But since it appears that scientists are especially sensitive to their modes of gratification and to the very personality traits that have made them become scientists, one must look very carefully at anything that tampers with and changes these systems of reward. Any such change will make Big Scientists people of different temperament and personality from those we have become accustomed to as traditional among Little Scientists.

The new phase of science seems to have changed the system of gratification in two different ways. In one direction, we have introduced the reward of general social status and financial return where there was precious little before. In the other direction, we have caused the scientist to seek the approbation

[11] Very little reliable work has been published on the psychology of scientists. The only books known to me are Anne Roe, *The Making of a Scientist* (New York, Apollo Editions, Inc., Reprint A-23) and Bernice T. Eiduson, *Scientists: Their Psychological World* (New York, Basic Books, Inc., 1962).

of his peers in a different way. The man of Maxwell's equations was something not quite the same as he of the Salk vaccine. Though according to the mythology a scientist is supposed to be eternally moved only by innate curiosity about how things work and what they can do, there is nowadays a slightly different social mechanism whereby a man is led to feel his personal inspiration and mavericity acknowledged among other men as having triumphed over ambient conservatism and caution as well as over the secrecy of nature.

If this is true at the highest level, it is also plain that in less stratified regions the invisible colleges and all lesser groups confer status and the means of leading a good life. They exercise power, and, the more power one has in such a group, the more one can select the best students, tap the biggest funds, cause the mightiest projects to come into existence. Such power does not, of course, represent any selfish lust on the part of the scientist. Society is supporting this structure and paying for it more and more because the results of his work are vital for the strength, security, and public welfare of all. With everything said to be depending on him, from freedom from military attack to freedom from disease, the scientist now holds the purse-strings of the entire state.

I hope it is not overdramatic to compare the present position of our scientific leadership to that which has existed in other countries, and in this country at other times, among the groups that used to control the means of destiny. On occasions, military power has been overriding, and then the generals have been in control, behind each palace revolt and cabinet meeting. Elsewhere it has been finance and the control of capital that were the mainspring of the state and the implement of decision. Or, in legislative government, one has seen the vital place taken by men of legal training. In a democracy we are accustomed to finding the leadership taken by men emerging from all these fields that have been crucial to the world's destiny.

Until recently, the scientist, insofar as he played any useful role in matters of state, was a passive instrument to be consulted like a dictionary, to turn out the right answer on demand. Several scientists and nonscientists will believe that it is desirable to maintain in the face of all difficulty the proposition that the scientist should be "on tap but not on top." Without arguing the ethics of the case, one can point out that the positive feedback governing the power of scientists works against any such proposition. The increased status of scientists and scientific work makes them increasingly vital to the state and places the state increasingly in the position of putting technical decisions into technical hands.

However, I am arguing not so much for the assumption of control by scientists over matters within their technical expertise but rather that their new tendency to rise to the political front as representatives of a group of people who hold the purse-strings of our civilization is to be encouraged. In a saturation economy of science it is obvious that the proper deployment of resources becomes much more important than expensive attempts to increase them.

In Great Britain and the United States very few of the senators, congressmen, members of Parliament, and active politicians—less than 3 percent, in fact—have had any training in science or technology. Among deputies in the Supreme Council of the U.S.S.R., the figure now exceeds 25 percent,[12] and, though their machinery of government is very different

[12] According to a survey by Science Service reported editorially in *Science*, 132 (September 30, 1960), 885.

from ours, I take this as an indication of the way our own future may lie.

In the old days of Little Science there was tremendous reaction against political action by scientists. They were lone wolves; they valued their independence; on the whole they liked *things* but were not very good at *people*. Their pay-off was the approbation of peers, and they were not supposed to crave any sort of admiration from the man in the street or any social status within society. Whether they like it or not, they now have such status and an increasing degree of affluence. They have come within the common experience. When I first saw the comic-strip character of Superman, who had once looked so much like an all-American football player, metamorphosing before my very eyes into an all-American nuclear physicist, I felt that the old game was up, and that the President-after-next might well be an ex-scientist.

This is the credit side of the register which balances some of the other, not so good, changes already noticed in the first generation of new-style Big Science. The scientist is accepted by society and must shoulder his responsibility to it in a new way. The rather selfish, free expansion by exponentially increasing private property of scientific discoveries must be moderated when one is in the logistic state. Racing to get there before the next man might well be, in the long run, an impossibly irresponsible action.

It must surely be averred as a matter of principle that the country that has arrived at a full logistic maturity, saturated with science, must try to behave with maturity and wisdom; must give some guidance to the younger countries that are growing up around and gradually outstripping it in scientific superiority.

One of the things I think is happening is the maturing of a

certain responsible attitude among scientists analogous to that which, in almost prehistoric times, moved physicians toward the concept of the Hippocratic Oath. Contrary to popular belief, this happened not because doctors were unusually dedicated or public-spirited people but because they were all too easily held personally responsible by their customers for poison, malpractice, and so on. The scientist has had a much harder time in arriving at this, for his customer has usually been the state rather than an individual. His guilt has been in the eyes of the world rather than in those of an individual. Here I refer not only to such matters as nuclear testing and fallout but also to a general question of what service science is rendering for the common good and for the improvement of man's higher understanding. Invisible colleges and groups now have the power to cast out their "poisoners and abortionists," and withdraw from them the old protective cloak of disinterestedness that was proper in the days of Little Science.

It is most heartening to find that on the whole, sundry much-publicized examples notwithstanding, the world body of scientists has been remarkably unanimous in political evaluations during recent years, and consistent in public action in an age of Big Science. Robert Gilpin's recent analysis [13] of this consistency makes a most hopeful document.

Scientists have hardly yet begun to realize that they hold in their own hands a great deal of power that they have hardly used. The ranks of senior scientists and key administrators of science have now swelled to the point where I think it will not be long before some of the good ones begin to enter politics rather more forcibly. We need such men, on the national scene

[13] Robert Gilpin, *American Scientists and Nuclear Weapons Policy* (Princeton, Princeton University Press, 1962).

and on the international scene. We need them for the internal reconstruction of the entire social fabric of science and for the external problems of science in the service of man.

It is my hope that in these lectures, beyond my own prides and prejudices in interpreting the data, I have shown that a whole series of annoyances and difficulties in scientific manpower and its literature are part of a single process in which at last we find a change in the state of science the like of which we have not seen for 300 years. The new state of scientific maturity that will burst upon us within the next few years can make or break our civilization, mature us or destroy us. In the meantime we must strive to be ready with some general understanding of the growth of science, and we must look for considerable assumption of power by responsible scientists, responsible within the framework of democratic control and knowing better how to set their house in order than any other men at any other time.

INDEX